New England in Focus:

The *Arthur Griffin* Story

Herbert A. Kenny and Damon Reed

Introduction by
John Updike

An Arthur Griffin Book 1995

ISBN 0-9642819-0-2
First Printing

Also by Arthur Griffin

The Boston Book (with Esther Forbes)

Village Greens of New England (with Louise Andrews Kent)

New England

New England Revisited

Arthur Griffin's New England: The Four Seasons

CREDITS

Book and Jacket Design by Lily M. Yamamoto, LMY Studio, Inc., Winchester, Massachusetts 01890

For the use of selections from copyrighted material, we are indebted to the following publishers and copyright proprietors:

Reprinted courtesy of Associated Press/Wide World Photos: "Upside down tree."

Reprinted courtesy of *The Boston Globe:* photo-stories and magazine covers from *The Boston Globe Rotogravure;* Jimmy Foxx series and Ignatz Paderewski; articles by V. O. Jones, "A 56-Year Wait," "Beacon Hill Ski Trail," "Dad Joins the Navy."

Courtesy © Eastman Kodak Company: The Eastman Kodak Colorama and the first Griffin photo sold to Eastman Kodak, 1948.

Used with permission. Hachette Filipacchi Magazines, Inc. Copyright 1994: *Boating* Magazine cover, December 1969.

Excerpts from *The Boston Book* by Arthur Griffin and Esther Forbes. Copyright © 1947 by Arthur L. Griffin and Esther Forbes Hoskins, © renewed 1974 by Arthur Griffin and Linwood M. Erskine, Jr. Reprinted by permission of Houghton Mifflin Company. All rights reserved.

From *Assorted Prose* by John Updike. Copyright © 1960 by John Updike. Reprinted by permission of Alfred A. Knopf, Incorporated. Originally appeared in *The New Yorker:* "Hub Fans Bid Kid Adieu."

Reprinted courtesy of Libbey • Owens • Ford Company, Incorporated: Libbey • Owens • Ford Glass advertisements

Reprinted courtesy of the Massachusetts Municipal Association: covers of *Massachusetts Selectman, Municipal Forum,* and *Municipal Advocate.*

New England Mutual Life Insurance Company. © 1958 Annual Report of New England Mutual Life Insurance Company. Reprinted with permission.

Reprinted courtesy of NYNEX Information Resources Company: the New England Telephone Company directory covers.

Life Magazine cover reprinted courtesy, Arthur Griffin, *Life* Magazine © Time Warner.

Reprinted courtesy of *The Winchester Star:* Art Illman photographs; articles "Golden Shovel" and "The Big One."

Reprinted from *The Saturday Evening Post,* with permission: "Face of America" selections; "They've Built 3000 Ships by Hand;" "A Picture Story That Took a Year to Do."

Reprinted courtesy of *Yankee* Magazine: "My 10 Favorite Spots in New England."

For the use of photographs taken by people other than Arthur Griffin we are truly grateful. In a few instances the photographers were "innocent bystanders," asked to take a photograph of Arthur with his own equipment. To all the unknown photographers and to those whose lives and names have long passed, we say thank you.

We are indebted to the following friends and photographers:

Art Illman: Frontmatter vi; Chapter 1, page 13; Chapter 2, page 30.

Polly Lee Griffin: Chapter 1, page 1; Chapter 2, page 27.

Carlyjane Watson: Chapter 1, page 7.

Larry Williams: Chapter 1, page 9, "Ribbon-cutting;" Chapter 6, page 71.

Michael J. Ryan: Chapter 1, page 12.

Richard L. Morton: Chapter 1, page 14.

Claire Kress: Chapter 2, page 15.

Claire Griffin: Chapter 2, page 21; Chapter 5, page 55; Chapter 8, page 95, Arthur; Chapter 9, page 103; Chapter 10, page 111.

Don Guy: Chapter 2, page 22.

Jimmy Krigman: Chapter 4, page 39.

Art Mogur: Chapter 8, page 95, Griffin and Boyer.

Jackie Greene: Chapter 10, page 115.

All color photographs made on KODAK Kodachrome and Ektachrome Daylight Film

DEDICATION

*I wish to dedicate my sixth and
perhaps last book to the hundreds of
wonderful, kind, and loving people
I have enjoyed meeting, photographing
and working with, world-wide, over
the past six decades.*

I want to express my personal gratitude to all of you who have helped make the Arthur Griffin Center for Photographic Art a reality. It would not have been built on the shore of Judkins Pond if it were not for the support of hundreds of people who helped in every way they could . . . people who donated to our endowment; people who refused payment for work on the design, construction, landscaping and maintenance of the Center and its grounds; people who guided us through all the red tape in getting our Center under way; and all the citizens of Winchester who have loaned a magnificent parcel of town land so the Center could be built in their and our community.

My deep appreciation is also extended to all of you who will continue to support our non-profit foundation as sponsors, donors, members, volunteers, trustees, directors, visitors and, of course, photographers. With a broad offering of workshops, talks, and exhibitions by acclaimed and aspiring artists, the Center hopes to provide varied and exciting programs while furthering an understanding of and appreciation for historic and contemporary photography. Please join us.

It is my hope that more and more people of all ages will come to know the excitement of photography — as journalism, art, science, or commerce. Come visit often. From myself, wife Polly and daughter Lee, our deepest appreciation to you all.

September 12, 1994

Arthur Griffin
The Arthur Griffin Center
for Photographic Art
67 Shore Road
Winchester, Massachusetts 01890

PROLOGUE

Once the Arthur Griffin Center for Photographic Art was opened, I was asked to write an autobiography, the life behind the thousands of photographs. An autobiography is an undertaking for a very brave person or a very vain one. I have my share of vanity, but not that much courage, so I asked two friends to join me in the undertaking. I asked Herbert A. Kenny, author, journalist and old friend, to write the biographical essays to accompany the chapters and individual photographs. I also asked Damon Reed, writer and editor, curator and new friend, to create a book that would further the public's awareness of our wonderful photography center just 12 miles from Boston. Together we have all selected photographs and stories, shared ideas and words, and enjoyed putting this book together.

There is a sense in which I am my photographs and certainly my stories. This book of photographs and tales is, therefore, in a way, autobiographical, as I take you on an armchair trip through New England and many other photogenic areas of the world I have visited during the past sixty-five years, on photographic assignments or in personal pursuit.

Over the years some friends have said, only half-joking, "Look at that Griffin. He travels around the world snapping pictures and never works." I have a stock answer, "You've no idea how tired my finger gets after a long hot day of snapping pictures. I can hardly wait to wrap it around a cold glass of beer."

My friends were partly right. When you do what you like you never really work, for your work is your play, and all the better that you get well paid for it. My life in that regard has been enviable. I have been fortunate in my choice of a career in that it has never seemed like work. Of course, being self-employed, I put in more hours per day than I ever would have for an employer. All absorbing and satisfying, mentally and physically, it surpassed the outright pursuit of pleasure. These pages are about a life which, within human limits, has been as happy as anyone has the right to ask.

To show my friends that it hasn't been all work and no play, I have included a variety of photographs and stories, some personal and some, I trust, amusing. The task of selecting these photographs from a life of more than 90 years and a career of 60 plus, proved as hard work as I have ever known, for no sooner had I selected one than I remembered yet another that asserted an equal right to inclusion. I consoled myself that those omitted may well end up on the walls of the Center in exhibitions.

For me, New England offers more for photographers, artists and lovers of beauty than any other area of its size in the world, so it will come as no surprise that the majority of the pictures I have chosen for this book will be local. There was much enjoyment in their taking.

I know New England like the feel of my camera. I have been over **her** highways and up the back dirt roads, cow paths and country lanes, and have walked the shores of many harbors, inlets and creeks. Over the years I have driven an average of 25,000 miles a year building up a tremendous file of black and white as well as color photographs, trying to catch the unique beauty of New England. My ambition, simply stated, has been to bring happiness through my pictures, to feel that the world was a bit better off for my having done what I did.

I have been lucky in my friends, but mostly in the love and help of two understanding wives. I have been given much and those who are given much are under an obligation to give in return. I hope that the joy in my pictures will bring pleasure for years and that the Arthur Griffin Center for Photographic Art will prosper and give pleasure. I hope too that this inescapably autobiographical book will make the Center better known and further its contributions to the many communities and individuals it welcomes and serves.

Arthur Griffin

Winchester, Massachusetts

September 12, 1994

PREFACE

Mayflower II

This is a book about art—the art of living fully, for a long lifetime. It is about the 1930s through the 1950s when photography entered the commercial mainstream with a rush of new materials, equipment, and opportunities. It is about a moment in time when New England seemed to be, in the words of poet David McCord, "the authorized version of America." Finally it is about a man with the foresight to recognize new opportunities, the wisdom to follow his own shifting interests, and the courage to be always himself.

Arthur Griffin's name may never be found in the annals of the world's great artists, but that was never his intention. In fact, he never put the word 'art' to his work until the naming of the museum he founded: The Arthur Griffin Center for Photographic Art. Though he began his journey as an artist, his routes were to commerce and a large and appreciative public, ultimately world-wide.

To put into 128 pages the life and work of such a man is no simple task. He has already published five books, lived more than 90 years and accumulated more than 75,000 pieces of photographic and journalistic history. But it is enjoyable and enlightening, for behind most images lie tales of history, people, and adventure, as told by Arthur Griffin, photographer and *raconteur*. These tales and photographs are ultimately about the passing of an era, one lived to the hilt and documented well by one of its vital travelers.

In selecting examples of his work, we have included those that reflect both the photographic limitations of an era and the technical wizardry required of Arthur to create the images he sought. He made bromoil prints in 1932, a time when photographers often tried to make their photographs, through inventive printing techniques, look like paintings. He created "action" shots of Jimmy Foxx and Andrea Mead when film was slow and high speed repetitive exposures just emerging.

Many Griffin images were produced and reproduced at a time when mass printing was still in its infancy. We have included *The Boston Globe*'s original rotogravure covers rather than Griffin's original photographs for the covers. As fourth generation prints, they are not crisp and clear photographs but documents of a photojournalistic era. The same may be said of much of the early color work reproduced in these pages. Rather than correcting or altering his early commercial color work, we have, in most cases, reproduced the cover, story, or advertisement as it has survived into 1994.

The wonderful color shots of a youthful Ted Williams, taken with "new" film Eastman Kodak sent to Griffin in '39, the black and white shots of Boston and her "generations," and Griffin's classic color landscapes were also selected to reveal the impact of time and technology on photojournalism, the human spirit and New England.

Some pictures we had to include because their stories simply could not be missed in this light-hearted look at Arthur's life and work. Some we have had to leave out . . . his march across thin ice at the age of 88 to get the proper angle for a picture of two visiting swans with his museum's grist mill in the background, a shot that might have turned into his "swan song" as ice cracked all around him as he gingerly headed for shore . . . or his harrowing experience aboard the aging wooden yacht, the Sea Doll, that sailed 100 miles to greet the replica of the *Mayflower* on its historic journey to Plymouth only, on its return, to have both engines quit requiring the tow of a navy destroyer out of the main shipping lanes to the Nantucket Lightship, where a fierce storm, for 14 hours, harrassed them and their new tow, the *U. S. Coast Guard*, cutting three times the enormous tow line and rendering most of the passengers ill, while Griffin, undaunted, crawled to the pitching bow to try, still again, to reattach the towline tossed by the U.S.C.G.!

Through Arthur's pictures and stories, through this brief look at his career, family and fun, we can know and enjoy this ageless New England photographer. And ultimately, through the photographic center that bears his name, we can all appreciate his passion for life, photography and his New England home.

Herbert A. Kenny and Damon Reed

GRIFFIN IN PERSON

It is all very well to look at the exquisite photographs, and to peruse the biographical facts, but this still leaves unaccounted for the presence, the charisma, the visible lust for life that has packed ninety unrepentant years onto Arthur's trim 5 foot 9 inch frame. The frame jiggles up and down, slightly, even in repose, tremulous with energy to hasten on to the next task, encounter, or, on the golf course, stroke. I have known Arthur most extensively on the golf course, his beloved Winchester links, where he beckoned me years ago, on the (false) rumor that I could help him land one of the prizes in a summer member-guest tournament. One year, thanks mostly to our skilled teammates, our foursome did finish in the money; heading toward my car and the hazards of negotiating Route 128 in the twilight, I directed Arthur to spend my share wisely, and he bought me a pair of pink-plaid polyester golf slacks that only he could wear without mortification. The odd thing is, they fit very nicely — they feel good — but I dare wear them seldom. When I do put them on, I abruptly know, for the second before natural embarrassment sweeps in, what it feels like to be Arthur Griffin. It feels like a lightning rod just after being hit by lightning, and still tingling.

Being Arthur Griffin would prematurely age most anyone else, but for Arthur it has been the passage to eternal youth. Who else, well into his eighties, would persevere through the bureaucratic brambles of small-town conservatism in order to bestow upon Winchester a grist mill filled with photographic treasure? Who else into his tenth decade would be cooking up this opulent album, this brimming yet inadequate record of his feats and flashes of photographic inspiration. Still cooking, that's Arthur. His inner tingle translates into an outer twinkle, a steady glimmer of good-humored excitement between the frosty goatee and the bill of his jaunty Greek captain's cap. When he speaks, there is sometimes a blur around a consonant or two, produced by excessive electricity, and eagerness to get on to the next utterance. On the golf course, there isn't a cart fast enough for him, and in an age of ponderous Nicklausian meditation Arthur would be for younger golfers the ideal model of dispatch. No sooner has he hopped out of the cart than the ball is scuttling up the fairway; no sooner has he assumed his putting stance than the ball is speeding toward the hole. If he sometimes takes a lot of shots to get to the green, it is no doubt because fewer would have left him with all that energy still to burn up; there should be in Winchester two golf courses, one on top of the other, so he could play them both simultaneously.

And I should add that Arthur can write too. More than one contributor to *Arthur Griffin's New England: The Four Seasons* noticed how much livelier than his or her own essay was Arthur's laconic yet vividly factual account of when and where and how he took the picture. God is in the details, they say; certainly photographic excellence stems from attention to details. That, and a willingness to seize the moment. At seizing moments Arthur Griffin is a veteran expert, and here are some of those he seized. He has caught on film the New England we all would like to think we live in; but perhaps only he really has lived in it, with a friendly fury that has rendered him ageless.

John Updike
March 7, 1994

TABLE OF CONTENTS

Polly Griffin, Sandy Rodgers and Whitney Gay, trustees of the Arthur Griffin Center, observing the "photographer on the roof."

A DREAM COMES TRUE

The Arthur Griffin Center for Photographic Art is a tribute to a man whose life has been about imagination and extra effort spiced with a touch of Yankee persistence and irreverence. Founded in Winchester, Massachusetts in 1992, the center is named for New England's "Photographer Laureate," Arthur Griffin, who spent more than sixty years as a photographic journalist on assignments that took him around the world and into the company of the renowned.

Arthur Griffin is not an ordinary man and never has been. His capacity for living life fully, even at 90, continues unabated. Artist, photographer, entrepreneur, pioneer and *raconteur extraordinaire*, "Griff" as he was known for many years, was fortunate to play a significant role in the emerging and merging fields of photography and journalism. His career in photojournalism and commercial photography, and his work with the rapidly developing and improving tools of the trade, both reflected and led numerous changes taking place in the 1930s through the 1960s.

The photography center that bears Griffin's name houses a legacy to which no ordinary man or woman could aspire and reflects a dream no ordinary man could envision.

- One of New England's first "cameramen" and photojournalists.

- First cameraman to use 35 millimeter for all black-and-white work.

- New England staff photographer for *Life* and *Time* magazines.

- Charter member of Boston Press Association, National Press Photographers Association, and American Society of Media Photographers.

- Photographer recognized by the Zeiss company with a national tour, in 1939, of 51 black and white photographs of New England's people, culture and commerce.

- Contributor to *Colliers, The Saturday Evening Post, Yankee, Holiday* and other national magazines for over 50 years.

- Pioneer in sports and landscape color photography:
  - First color photographs taken of Ted Williams, 1939.
  - First color photographs to appear in *The Boston Globe*, 1940.
  - First color photographs to appear in *The Saturday Evening Post*, 1945.
  - First color photographs to appear in *Yankee* Magazine, 1959.

- Worked with Eastman Kodak Company for 25 years experimenting with new color film and enjoying advertisement and stock assignments worldwide.

- Documented the life and spirit of Boston in *The Boston Book*, published in 1947 by Houghton Mifflin, with photographs by Griffin and text by Pulitzer Prize recipient Esther Forbes.

"Use a little imagination and create something that will not be just a record of a beautiful place. The extra effort and thought will result in something with some of you in it."

New England Revisited
September 12, 1966

- Set the standard for all classic color New England landscapes and documented the passing of an era in New England with the publication of the first full color pictorial book of New England landscapes, *New England* (published September 12, 1962), followed by *New England Revisited* (1966) and *Arthur Griffin's New England: The Four Seasons* (1980).

- Integrated documentary, commercial and landscape photography, in color and in black and white, for more than 60 years.

- Founded The Arthur Griffin Center for Photographic Art, a non-profit center in Winchester, Massachusetts that, through the generosity of friends, neighbors and photography buffs, opened its doors to the public on September 12, 1992.

The Arthur Griffin Center for Photographic Art is now home to the Griffin Collection, more than 75,000 negatives, transparencies, rotogravures, black and white vintage prints, dye transfer prints, magazine spreads and covers, and the paraphernalia of his trade and life. It is a vast and varied collection that reflects significant developments taking place during the 1920s, '30s and '40s in photography as an art form and a field of commerce. And it reveals the shifting interests, styles and career choices that were inevitable for Arthur Griffin.

The pages that follow provide but a glimpse of Griffin's life and work. Each decade and chapter of his life, and of this book, tells of imagination, opportunity and what Arthur would call "luck." The following stories and photographs by Arthur, of Ignatz Paderewski, Jimmy Foxx, and Andrea Mead exemplify well his imagination and his ability to make the impossible quite possible.

My Most Challenging Photograph

"On May 11, 1939 the great pianist Ignatz Paderewski came to the Boston Opera House. He was almost blind. He insisted that no flashbulbs, no stage lighting be used while he was on stage. Just dim lighting. The hall was full to overflowing, with fans on the stage behind a low backdrop. The *Globe* had bought a whole box, in which I set up my tripod and my small German 35mm camera with a telephoto lens. I believe I was the only newspaper photographer in the country using a 35mm exclusively at that time. "Black and white film was very slow then. I knew I would have to have a very long exposure and, with his head moving most of the time, it would be almost impossible to get a clear picture. But I had to get something. So I tried something I had never done before . . . or since. I held the program in front of the lens, then opened the shutter and left it open. When I thought that his head might be still, I removed the program. When it moved, I put the program back. (I could tell when his head returned to about the same position with a design on the backdrop. Without this design I would have been out of business.) When his head came back, I took the program off, building up the exposure. I repeated this procedure for two rolls of film, 72 pictures. Out of all that I only got two fairly good pictures. The *Globe* featured the picture on the front page and, at the time of Paderewski's death in 1941, the photo again appeared in the rotogravure section. The photo won a few prizes."

Ignatz Paderewski, May 11, 1939

JIMMY FOXX in a STEP by STEP

Jimmy Foxx, July 31, 1938

This black and white series of the famous Jimmy Foxx, Boston's slugging first baseman, was taken in 1938. Griffin, always experimenting with film and cameras, borrowed a new Zeiss camera from an old friend, Ralph Harris. Unlike most other 35mm cameras of the time, that had to be turned ahead to the next negative after each picture, the new German "robot" allowed high speed repetitive exposures. Griffin made twelve separate pictures of Foxx which he assembled into this panorama of Foxx reaching first base on his home run hit at Fenway Park. The advertisements and some of the advertisers on the famous left field wall may be gone, but the score board still looks much the same as it did back in 1938.

"HERE'S WHAT AMERICAN LEAGUE PITCHERS are seeing in their nightmares . . . Jimmy Foxx, Boston's slugging first baseman, clouting the ball and starting towards first. On the extreme left is Bill Dickey, the Yank's catcher, vainly waiting for a ball that never got across the plate. From the position of Foxx's bat and the ball just leaving it, the pitcher evidently tried to whistle a shoulder high inside ball . . . . Foxx's bat meets it and then follows through. Then Foxx is off for first, his eye still on the ball to see whether he can safely try for second. The two shots on the left are interesting because they bring out clearly the fact that Foxx gets his tremendous power from his wrists, depending comparatively little on his body weight, or even his shoulders. Most long-distance sluggers, notably Babe Ruth, got their whole body into their blows, but Foxx can park a ball out of the lot by just cocking his wrists."

V.O. Jones
The Boston Globe
July 31, 1938

ICTURE after WHALING the BALL

GLOBE STAFF PHOTOS, ARTHUR GRIFFIN

 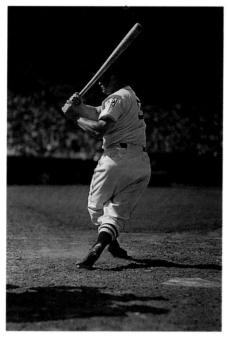

The tools of the trade were changing rapidly and commercial color film was in its infancy. Kodak often asked Griffin to try their new products, including film. These two color photographs of Foxx were taken in 1938 when Foxx was fast, color film slow and good action shots almost impossible. Griffin took these color shots a year before making his famous Ted Williams portraits. The transparencies of Foxx and Williams, "lost" for 50 years, reemerged during planning for the new photography center.

Andrea Mead, January 1954

Vermont Flyer

"In 1951, I photographed Andrea Mead, a young girl from Rutland, Vermont. She was a terrific skier and had great possibilities of being on the next U.S. Olympic team. I made some shots of Andrea and sold this picture to the *Globe*. Needless to say, the forecast on Andrea was accurate and she won the Gold Medal, the first American to do so.

"In January, 1954, on assignment with *Colliers*, I made a series of night action shots of Andrea, a year after she had won the gold. What wasn't in the *Colliers* story is that this was probably the first time that multiple exposures were made on a 4″ × 5″ Ektachrome transparency. I had to make it at night. My wife was at the base of the hill with my 4″ × 5″ Linhof camera on a tripod. I was up the hill with a strobe light. The camera shutter was open and my wife was holding a plate holder over the lens. As "Andy" approached the flags, I would call my wife to take the plate off the lens. Then I would fire the strobe light, just as Andy came through the gates. Andy would stop, waiting until I moved to the next set of flags with the strobe. We repeated the procedure until she had been through all five sets. There was no concern about over-exposure as there was no light on the hill except when the strobe flashed. I shot about six series like this running up and down to be in the right place to fire the strobe light as Andy came through the gates. My exertions had me sweating despite the freezing weather. My wife's less active role had left her frozen. Andy simply took it all in stride, enjoying what she loved best, skiing."

In 1987 Griffin offered to the town of Winchester a center that would serve both as a museum for his work and as an active photography center. His determination to have the museum in the town he loved, and to have it an autonomous enterprise, was typical of him. A most gregarious man by nature, given to dress of flamboyant style, a *raconteur* despite a life-long stammer, with a penchant for practical jokes and pranks, he asked only that the town provide a suitable site for the museum he would build. He would manage the project and pay for the building himself.

Five years of negotiation, deliberation and inevitable exasperation followed as questions of aesthetics, environmental protection, financial responsibility, design and construction were thrashed out in public, in the State legislature, in the press, and in committee meetings. Finally on the floor of that wonderful New England invention, the town meeting, Arthur won overwhelming approval for the Arthur Griffin Center and a 99-year lease on its present site, Judkins Pond.

The timeless and picturesque village of Winchester is an ideal site for Griffin's Center. Home to Griffin and his family for more than 58 years, it is located only 15 minutes from Boston, the city that provided Griffin with his start first in commercial art and later in photography. Boston is also a city that could well claim to be the fountainhead of photography in the United States through its long history of photographic tinkers, adventurers and artists.

The story of the Arthur Griffin Center for Photographic Art can best be told in pictures.

Finally on September 12, 1991, the golden shovel was put to use. Onlookers recalled that Griffin was so anxious the first day, he dug up the entire foundation. Actually, Griffin's daughter, Lee, had buried a bottle of champagne in the ground for Griffin to dig up. Unfortunately, someone knocked over the shovel, which was standing next to the buried champagne and replaced it in a different spot. Griffin carefully dug up the first shovelful, as to not break the champagne bottle he knew was waiting in the ground. It wasn't there. He tried again. No luck. Soon he was furiously digging up a truck-load of dirt.

The Winchester Star, *"A Dream Comes True,"* September 12, 1992

Groundbreaking: September 12, 1991

Arthur had a great deal of support for the Center, none more consistent and valued than that of his wife Polly. Also an artist, Polly enjoys a reputation for fine silhouettes known for their keen likenesses. Her silhouette of Arthur, converted to the Center's weather vane, is also found in its Library.

Construction: 1991-1992

Final inspection of the Center by builder, Charles Westgate, The Royal Barry Wills team, and Sandy Rodgers, trustee, who, along with dozens of others gave generously of their time and resources.

Bill Dingwell, trustee, installs sign.

Ribbon cutting.

In 1938, Arthur prepared a picture story for *Life* magazine about a young architect and his practical and historic design for the "Cape Cod" house. Royal Barry Wills was his name and, within a year after the article appeared, his career took off. Fifty years later, his son Richard acknowledged that early gift of Arthur's '38 story by designing the Griffin Center for Arthur, at no charge. Wills' generosity was echoed again and again by those who only wished to say "thank you" to Arthur or "good luck" to what they knew was an important contribution to the Greater Boston community and to the field of photography.

ARTHUR GRIFFIN
CENTER FOR PHOTOGRAPHIC ART WINCHESTER, MASSACHUSETTS
ROYAL BARRY WILLS ASSOCIATES BOSTON, MASSACHUSETTS
A R C H I T E C T S

A Dream Comes True: September 12, 1992

The Arthur Griffin Center, a replica of an old field stone grist mill, appropriately reflects the historic and the contemporary. Its handsome barnwood and fieldstone architecture is reminiscent of New England's rich heritage; the lazy water wheel of the gristmill a reminder of the many old mills powered by the Aberjona River as it flowed through Winchester.

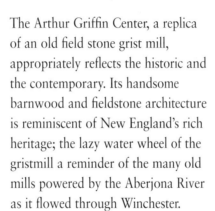

Looking into the Library

The Main Gallery

The 1500-square foot modern gallery, with state of the art lighting and movable walls, exhibits the work of aspiring and acclaimed fine art and commercial photographers. Each year, to mark Arthur's birthday and the opening of the Center, a major exhibition of his work is displayed in the Main Gallery.

The Gristmill and Library provide an opportunity to view, year round, Griffin's own images of New England's landscape, people and culture.

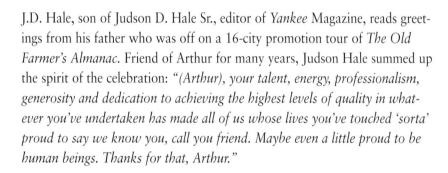

J.D. Hale, son of Judson D. Hale Sr., editor of *Yankee* Magazine, reads greetings from his father who was off on a 16-city promotion tour of *The Old Farmer's Almanac*. Friend of Arthur for many years, Judson Hale summed up the spirit of the celebration: *"(Arthur), your talent, energy, professionalism, generosity and dedication to achieving the highest levels of quality in whatever you've undertaken has made all of us whose lives you've touched 'sorta' proud to say we know you, call you friend. Maybe even a little proud to be human beings. Thanks for that, Arthur."*

The National Press Photographers Association, Inc. also recognized Arthur's "more than forty years of service in newsphotography." Charles H. Cooper, Executive Director of the NPPA, sent a letter that read in part, *"We would like to further salute you on this your 90th birthday, a significant milestone in your illustrious career as a Life Member and Charter Member of this association, a pioneer in so many ways as a photographer, and for your accomplishments and contributions to your profession."*

Griffin's 90th birthday, September 12, 1993, marked the first anniversary of the Griffin Center and welcomed a major exhibition of his early work in the Main Gallery, "The Photographic Legacy of Arthur Griffin, 1933 – 1993."

Arthur Griffin's 90th Birthday: September 12, 1993

The old pot-bellied stove, now at the Center, was in the Griffin home for many years, a source of heat during World War II and an integral part of many Griffin escapades, Christmas cards and gatherings. Arthur's first wife, Claire, who died in 1977, played a key role during those early years as Arthur's personal and professional partner and helpmate. In 1979, Arthur was fortunate to find Polly Lee Howe, his new wife and partner. Together they enjoy a quiet moment in front of the old pot bellied stove at The Griffin Center.

Arthur and Polly Griffin, 1992

A wonderful group of people is responsible for the success of the Arthur Griffin Center. Businesses have donated enthusiastically. Friends of photography and of Arthur have given graciously for our endowment. Others have donated time and energy to help make the Center the ongoing cultural concern that it is. We thank you, each and every one.

Arthur Griffin is an artist, a character, and a town asset all wrapped up in one. On his birthday, the trustees and all of us helping to make his vision a reality salute him. We thank him for bringing a venture totally new and refreshing to the town, and pledge, as our birthday gift to him, to continue the work of bringing exciting and educational photography and new programs and visitors to the community for the benefit of all.

Court Crandall,
Chairman, Board of Trustees

September 12, 1993

Arthur in studio, 1993

THE WORLD ACCORDING TO ARTHUR

Arthur Griffin was born September 12, 1903, in the city of Lawrence, Massachusetts, the fourth of eight children. His father, Andrew J. Griffin, was born in Edinburgh, Scotland while his parents were on visit there from Ireland. Arthur's mother, Mary Dietel, was born in Lawrence shortly after her parents arrived from Germany. Lawrence, then a model New England mill city, was at the height of its prosperity, with immigrants pouring in from dozens of different countries. But change was coming and Arthur's future would lie elsewhere.

Photography was passing from infancy to adolescence at the turn of the century. A month or two after Arthur's birth, Arthur Stieglitz, one of the major figures in the early history of American photography, founded the magazine *Camera Work*. In the same year, Joseph Pulitzer, the publisher who fathered mass circulation of newspapers, gave Columbia University the money to found its celebrated school of journalism. Four years later the Lumiere brothers, French film pioneers, announced the birth of a method of practical color photography. Miles and years apart, these developments would play an important part in Arthur Griffin's life.

Arthur's childhood laid in a store of memories and experiences that taught well the values and vagaries of life. The famous Lawrence workers' strike of 1912, that brought "the worsted capital of the world" to the attention of the world, got Arthur's attention as well. Strikers facing soldiers' bayonets; the disappearance of poor school chums, shipped out of state to escape harm or starvation. He remembers well the influenza epidemic of 1918–1919 with its hundreds of tents serving as hospitals; its ravaging and devastating toll on an already poor and deteriorating city.

This was also a childhood that taught the importance of accepting and using your gifts, no matter what their packaging. Arthur's package included a stammer and stutter that at times brought him great discomfort. But it also brought opportunities throughout his life he couldn't imagine as a young boy. His parents were convinced that he would receive more understanding and sympathy from the teaching sisters at a nearby parochial school. There he discovered his talent for art and accepted his stutter.

"Leave your car at home, hop over the back-yard fence and discover your neighborhood."

Boston Sunday Globe
April 19, 1943

one summer. At that time Arthur was employed at a job that gave him the use of a small smithy. Here he hammered out hardware fittings and a chandelier for the new lodge that could boast a chandelier but still no running water. A design for one of his early Christmas cards was of the beloved lodge.

As a youngster in Lawrence, Arthur had always wanted to be an artist. In 1921, with the assistance of a paperboy scholarship, he began a two-year program in drawing at the New School of Design in Boston. For a young art student, commuting daily from Lawrence, it was an exciting place to be. It was also time to experiment. Always somewhat eccentric, Arthur now shunned the crew cuts of the age for the longer hair and colorful clothes of the artist. His indulgence in colorful and often flamboyant clothes persisted all his life and, with his Tyrolean and Greek hats, became his trademarks.

Left: *Andrew J. Griffin, Arthur's father, Everard the oldest child, and Mary Dietel Griffin, his mother.*
Right: *Arthur (on right) with his brother Frederick at their home on Rhine Street, Lawrence. Ten years after Arthur's birth and one block away, Leonard Bernstein, conductor and composer, was born. Years later both would be bracketed with some other celebrated Lawrence natives in a newspaper story about the city's distinguished sons.*
Far right: *Canobie Lake Cottage*

Arthur's childhood also ripened in him a robust curiosity and sense of play, and a love of beauty and of nature, framed by values for hard work and order. Arthur remembers well his self-educated father returning from a plumbing business, tired and dirty, only to emerge for dinner well-scrubbed and freshly attired. His patient mother, shining shoes, scrubbing faces, and carefully handling the finances and faith of her upwardly mobile family. Family outings to gather berries and fruits for preserving. Mason jars lined up on shelves in the cellar. A barrel of apples and crock of dill pickles. Flour by the barrel and fresh bread and pies every day. And finally a summer cottage of their own on the shore of a lake in nearby New Hampshire.

The Griffins spent many rollicking vacations at their Spartan Canobie Lake cottage that claimed neither running water nor indoor toilets. They had to walk two miles to a farm to buy milk and row across the lake in order to reach the trolley cars that took them to Lawrence and to any sizable stores. Their days were filled with getting water from the lake for cooking and cleaning, chopping wood, tending their garden, picking blueberries and raspberries, fishing, rowing, romping and always finding time for family pranks and projects.

Once the Griffin children began to depart for summer jobs and careers, they still managed to get back to their summer cottage. One of the older brothers bought three lots of land near the Griffin cottage and agreed to let his siblings build on one of them. Arthur's interest in design and art found an outlet in the brothers' project. He designed a stone lodge that they built in

Throughout his school years, his father remained eager for Arthur to follow his trade but his persuasions were not convincing. One day Mr. Griffin made a surprise visit to the school and asked to see his son. He was directed to a studio where he found Arthur intensely sketching a nude model. Arthur was unaware of his father's arrival until he heard, "So this is why you wanted to be an artist instead of a plumber. Does your mother know about this?" Soon after, Arthur, returning home from school with a large black portfolio under one arm, was greeted by his mother and her sewing circle. He tried sneaking in the back way but was heard and summoned to show his work. Arthur suggested strongly that they should wait until he had something good to show them but they were insistent. Rather than staying to endure their comments, he fled. "Judging by the sounds I heard, my work made impression enough." His technique was not the prime subject of discussion; but there was no aftermath.

Of Andrew Griffin, "Pa thought a plumber would put more food on the table."

Above left: *One of Arthur's early photographs, of his youngest brother John, was taken with lighting supplied by a flashlight held in John's lap.*
Above right: *Griffin in his art studio. Charcoal portrait, by Griffin, is of his friend Bill Cini.*

In 1923 Arthur received another scholarship for an extra year of study in commercial art at the New School of Design. Business in Boston was booming. Upon graduating, he opened a commercial art studio and quickly developed a number of repeat and loyal clients including some of the many publishers and advertising agencies headquartered in the city. In 1929 he was hired by the art department at *The Boston Globe* to work from 6:00 p.m. to 1:00 a.m. drawing illustrations for advertisements. His freelance activities continued.

In 1932, Arthur took a three-month leave from the *Globe* and toured Europe by train and bicycle. This trip kindled in Arthur a love of travel and cameras. The photographs he shot in Europe were the genesis of his photographic career. But he returned to the art department at the *Globe* and to his successful freelance art business. His photography would for a while be confined to informal work of his own: from the people of Boston, to his family and the mountains of New Hampshire.

Of Mary Griffin, "Ma encouraged me in my dreams of being an artist."

The summers in New Hampshire had developed in Arthur a love of the outdoors and of the natural world. He naturally took to hiking and skiing and, beginning in 1925 traveled frequently to the White Mountains of New Hampshire, long enjoyed by poets, artists and photographers. As early as 1862, Franklin White, a landscape painter turned photographer, made a midwinter nighttime ascent of the region's Mount Washington to make some glass plates for stereoscopic viewing, and was trapped for two days in the Summit house with two companions, narrowly escaping freezing to death. When they arrived at the then unoccupied Summit house, so deep was the snow and ice they had to enter by an attic window.

*Griffin's first hike up
Mt. Washington in 1925*

Arthur's Mount Washington experiences were sometimes poetic, sometimes perilous. On one occasion, he joined thousands for the annual spring trek into Mt. Washington's Tuckerman's Ravine, a favorite slope for veteran skiers, with a half-mile descent pitched far too steeply for beginners. His work more or less done, he closed his 4″ × 5″ view camera, put the smaller camera, a Medalist, around his neck and started down the steep slope, carefully placing his feet in toeholds in the icy surface while using the folded tripod for balance.

"Somehow," he recounts, "after just a few feet of maneuvering I slipped and started down the 45-degree, half-mile pitch, sliding on my backside. I tried to check my fall by digging my elbows into the snow but continued to tumble and slide at breakneck speed. Luckily I stopped before landing in a nest of rocks. I know I might have been killed, as many are. As it was I got out of it with badly scraped elbows . . . the price I paid for making the fastest downhill run of the day."

Tuckerman's Ravine

In 1934 Arthur was to witness first hand the greatest wind ever recorded by man. In early April, Arthur was on the mountain top with his friend, George Leslie, a member of the Appalachian Mountain Club. The weather was clear when they arrived but suddenly a sharp wind came up. The men went into the now famous Mt. Washington Observatory to ride out what they thought would be a brief blow. The wind rose and blew relentlessly. For four days a fierce storm raged bringing sustained winds of extreme velocities and leaving a treacherous hard, blue-ice casing over all surfaces. The observation station was threatened but three massive chains, that passed over the roof and anchored the building to the ground, held. The five men inside, two visitors

Top: *Griffin on summit of Mount Washington.*
Below: *After the Big Wind. Arthur's contribution to the affair had been to record the numbers called out to him by the Observatory crew and to sketch his companions. Once outside, he also shot some pictures that record a stark, frozen and magnificent Mt. Washington summit.*

The summit of Mt. Washington, taken by Griffin from an airplane, in the early 1940s. Mt. Washington (6288 feet), highest peak east of the Mississippi and north of the Carolinas, was first seen from the ocean as early as 1605. Its first recorded ascent was in 1642 by Darby Field and two Native Americans. Storms of incredible violence in the summer and winter months have taken many lives, four alone during the winter of 1994.

and a scientific crew of three, maintained a constant vigil as equipment blew off the roof and watched the recording stylus with astonishment. Attempts to check the equipment outdoors became dangerous and losing battles that finally had to be abandoned. Finally at 1:30 p.m. on April 12 they listened to the tone signals, actuated by the anemometer contacts, spelling out the record gusts of 231 mph, a record that remains unchallenged in 60 years throughout the world.

Life in the city was also busy and exciting. And for Arthur, mildly Bohemian. The Griffin studio, that he shared with a friend, became the Saturday night party headquarters for many of their friends. This was the era of Prohibition and the age of speakeasies, bootleggers and bathtub gin. It was also the era of Griffin's parties that became so popular and well-known he finally rented halls, hired orchestras and charged admission. For a period of five years, he staged four costume parties a year, one for each season, each with some madcap theme and each with an invitation designed by Arthur. "Only couples admitted; no stags; no tickets sold at the door; appropriate costumes required." Once underway, the enterprising Griffin found he was actually making money.

Invitations

The parties played an important role for Arthur — an introduction in January, 1934, to Claire Kress whom he would marry the following October. For his New Year's party he selected the Longwood Cricket Club in Brookline, famous as the birthplace of lawn tennis in the United States. Franklin Delano Roosevelt had been elected President and Arthur called this costume ball, the "New Deal Review." Despite the Depression, it was the most profitable party he ever ran: he made five times his *Globe* salary and found the woman who was to be his wife and partner for 43 years.

The new bride and groom sent a wedding photograph to their parents that was definitely not by Bachrach of Boston. Their joke was not well received by their parents but loved by their friends. It was one of the early antics shared and enjoyed by Claire and Arthur, one of many yet to come.

Claire and Arthur, the new bride and groom, 1934

Shortly after their marriage, Arthur and Claire moved to Winchester, to a home designed by Arthur. In the years to come he would design and build much of their hard wood furniture by hand — "Power tools? What are power tools?" asks Griffin. In about 1952 a tree blew down on their roof and instead of repairing the roof they raised it and built a room with an "embossed-copper" ceiling made of apple-packing trays. Theirs was a lively and inventive home, in decor and antics.

The Griffins sent Christmas cards each season to friends and associates around the world, designed by one of them. They loved the pot bellied stove and couldn't resist these shots for their '42 card. To some friends they sent the picture of Arthur in the tub; to others the picture of Lee, their daughter. On several occasions friends, who didn't know the Griffins had sent two different cards, would remark on "that darling Griffin card" only to be chided, "What's so darling about Arthur in a tub?"

Among the many objects of the Griffins' love of fun were their Christmas trees, magnificently decorated but somehow always different and noteworthy. Upside down, slit in half, angled or created from copper, the Griffin trees became admired or scorned. Children from the neighborhood couldn't wait to see the Griffin tree. Over the years they were at the center of much press and many pranks.

A photograph of daughter Lee appeared in newspapers across the country. Don Guy of the Associated Press office in Boston photographed it, and "the AP sent the picture all over creation. We received notes from friends in Europe and Asia who had seen the picture in their local papers."

It happened one night . . .

"It was Christmas Eve in our Winchester home in the early 1940s and we had a visitor. He was an excellent neighbor, elderly, dignified and temperate. Let's call him Mr. Sedate. It was his custom to take one drink a year with his pals on Christmas Eve. This was the time, and he had had the drink.

"When he came into our house he stopped in the hall a full minute, regarding the living room scene. Our Christmas tree, lavishly decorated, hung from the fifteen foot high ridge pole. It was hung with little lights which flickered on and off. Furthermore, it was upside down, just to be different.

"Mr. Sedate stepped down into the living room and to a seat on the divan, between his wife and son. He said not a word; just stared at the tree.

"Finally he spoke: 'Mr. Griffin, that tree looks as if it's spinning around.' I replied, 'What, Mr. Sedate, what do you mean?' Silence for a few more minutes. Then: 'Mr. Griffin, it now looks as if it's upside down and the lights are going on and off. I'm going home.'

"He went but his wife and son stayed. They understood the situation a little better. In spite of his one drink, Mr. Sedate's observations had been accurate. The tree was, of course, upside down. It hung near an outlet from the heating system and it did spin back and forth, as the current of hot air struck it. And its little lights did flicker on and off."

Life was never dull for the Griffin family. In fact, it got zanier and livelier as Griffin, in 1946, left the *Globe* to become a freelance photographer. Through his many national contacts, more doors opened to Griffin ushering numerous and varied assignments and opportunities. In 1947 Houghton Mifflin published his first book, *The Boston Book*, with photographs by Griffin and text by Pulitzer Prize winner Esther Forbes. This was followed in 1948 with *Village Greens of New England*. Written by Louise Andrews Kent, author of books for children and adult readers, the book furthered Arthur's interest in publishing.

Arthur's freelance years also brought him work with more publications, more companies and more celebrities. During his years with the *Globe* and as a freelance photographer, he photographed hundreds of celebrities, many of whom would become close friends.

One celebrity was Gene Tunney, retired heavyweight champion of the world and avid fisherman. Their meeting occurred in Nova Scotia following an international tuna derby. Competitors were invited from throughout the world and there were more newspaper men there than fishermen. Yet not one tuna was caught. On the afternoon of the final day, Griffin saw Gene Tunney standing on the pier. "I quickly got off the boat, introduced myself and asked if he intended to fish the next day, even though the Derby was over. He invited me to join him and for three days I stayed with Tunney, catching plenty of action on camera but no fish. Finally on the third day Tunney had a strike and brought in a 606-pound tuna. It might well have been the winner in that scoreless derby. But what a great time we had . . . gourmet dinners at night and the start of a wonderful friendship that spanned many years and many miles. Eventually I persuaded Tunney to write a story about his battle with the tuna titled "My Toughest Fight." The story was eventually sold to Colliers.

Griffin with "the big one".

Griffin claims that the only time he had a rod in his hands was when he was heading for home port off Cuttyhunk where he had been taking pictures of six elder striped bass fishermen for *Holiday* magazine. "They had not one strike the whole day and we were all headed home. I was sitting along side my old friend Captain John Peterson who was trolling. Peterson asked me to hold his rod while he went to the "head." A minute later I was almost pulled out of the boat with a strike. With the advice of the other men, I brought in a 56-pound striped bass, much larger than any the elder bass statesmen had ever caught."

&

An article in the local newspaper reported the following week that "Mr. Griffin has no explanation for his amazing feat but feels that in the years he has been with fishermen, while working on assignments, he evidently picked up a great amount of experience in carefully watching the habits and techniques of his subjects . . . . All these years Griffin felt that he couldn't properly fish and take pictures at the same time, but knew that he could at least eat from his pictures which was more than he could do if his friends' success with rod and reel was a good example of what he might catch. Anyhow, last week he decided that this was the time, place, tide and moon to give his combination of assorted techniques a try. He did feel a bit let-down after catching the big one . . . but really thinks that fishing is a bit over-rated and not quite as difficult as it is cracked up to be and wonders if fishing with sling-shots or bow and arrow might not give the fish an even break."

The Winchester Star (date unknown)

Several people who knew Arthur well would refute his claim that he had never fished before, for they often saw his body and face, with rod in hand, in some of his own pictures. He in fact made many pictures of himself whenever it was the only way to get the shot he wanted. With a delayed shutter release, he had a few seconds to get "into position." With a few extra bright shirts, casual hats and fishing equipment in his car, he was ready for many of his own modeling needs.

"One day, while 'fishing' in the famous Battenkill River in Vermont, a game warden drove up, stopped and yelled across the river, 'Do you have a fishing license?' I yelled 'NO' and he instructed me to 'Get right out.' I carefully pulled in the line with the stone on it and said 'Now how could I catch a fish with a stone as bait?' He then noticed my tripod and camera, set with a delayed action release. A can of cold beer cooled him down just right."

Claire and Lee, 1940

Although Arthur continued to accept a variety of assignments, his interest turned increasingly to color photography and the landscape. For many years he put 25,000 miles on his car traveling the backroads of New England until he knew her coast, mountains and valleys as well as or better than anyone.

Over time his reputation as a fine New England landscape photographer took hold. In 1962, with his production of the first all color photographic book on New England, reviews hailed him as New England's "Photographer Laureate." *New England* was an immediate photographic, artistic and financial success, a success in which Arthur, Claire and Lee could share. They had developed and produced it as a team and, still as a team, they went on to create *New England Revisited*, published in 1966.

Arthur began work on a third book in the 1970's but his wife of 43 years became ill with cancer. Arthur shelved the book and all other work while he tended Claire in her long illness. She died in 1977.

On Arthur's 80th birthday, he prepared for his friends a collection of "Reminiscences." He wrote that the dedication of his first book, *New England*, "sums up pretty well the forty-three wonderful, exciting and interesting years we spent together."

"To Claire, The Best Camera Caddy in the World. The one who has helped carry equipment in many parts of the world, taken notes, names and locations. Packed bags for one night stands that went into weeks and comforted me while waiting for THAT special light or just SUN. In between all this she manages to take wonderful black and white photographs."

Arthur's 80th birthday musings included the other "gals in his life." His daughter Lee, by now a graduate of the Rhode Island School of Design and a freelance artist in Los Angeles, was "an integral part of the Griffin team, our projects, travels, and antics. She was and is a joy to be with."

He also spoke of his mother ". . . the most wonderful mother in the world. Only five feet tall and never weighing over 100 pounds, she was a dynamo and complete boss in her small home with eight kids."

Polly Howe Griffin

"Last but not at all least is Polly. Polly Howe married Bill Lee who was a next door neighbor of Claire in Lawrence when they were kids. Claire and I had named our daughter for Bill's parents whom we had been friends with for many years. After Bill's death, Polly was a widow for eight years. We had visited the Lees but I hadn't seen Polly for 15 years although we had kept in touch over the years with Christmas Cards. The year after Claire's death, after receiving Polly's annual Christmas Card, I called her for a dinner date. We discovered we had a great deal in common. Polly is now my sweet, talented wife."

Arthur and Polly's wedding announcement designed by Polly.

Christmas cards from the Griffins were now often sketched by Polly. Traveling was again frequent and eventful. An 80th birthday party for Arthur, organized by Polly and Lee, invited guests to "C-C-Come to M-M-My 80th B-B-Birthday P-Party."

Fellow artist, travel companion and humorist, Polly also became Arthur's partner in his quest for a photography center to house his collection. She worked at his side during the five years of negotiation and planning, lending her strength and warmth to the public image and to the complicated process. Her contributions to the Center have been many, the most visible the design of the weathervane, a silhouette of Arthur, that welcomes all to the Arthur Griffin Center.

Polly, Point Reyes National Park, California, 1988

Polly and Lee, Pemaquid Point, Maine, 1980

Now in his tenth decade, Arthur Griffin, the man under the cap, retains the energy and character of his youth. Throughout his life, his vision enabled him to set a course and profit by it. His child-like sense of fun drove him to pranks, antics and a flamboyance of dress that became his personal trademark. His untiring curiosity made him an eager world traveler and technical tinkerer. And his ease with and love of people opened doors, ultimately the doors of The Arthur Griffin Center for Photographic Art.

The man under the cap, 1993

1932: Europe on $1.00 a Day

Arthur Griffin's extensive and life-long traveling began soon after graduating from the New School of Design. In 1932 the United States still looked to France and Italy for direction in things aesthetic. Griffin, already employed in the art department of the *Globe* and living the life of a "mildly bohemian bon-vivant," looked to Europe for adventure and art.

The jaunty, mustached Griffin went as an artist, to see the museums of Europe, to sketch and photograph subjects he would work on later at home: fishing villages, quiet pastoral scenes, small villages and their inhabitants . . . themes and subjects embraced by Griffin throughout his career. He returned from Europe intrigued with photography as a possible art form.

Griffin carried the first camera he had ever owned, an Eastman Kodak Brownie, not the familiar box camera, but one with folding bellows. He had bought it from Thomas S. Baker, a fellow student who would become a distinguished water colorist. For back-up and experimentation he carried a German 3 1/4″ × 4 1/4″ view camera. Griffin had earlier experimented with the Brownie and with developing film in the dark room maintained by the Boston Camera Club at the Young Men's Christian Union on Boylston Street. It was here he culled both advice and stories from the "old-timers" and from members of the oldest camera club in the United States.

As was true throughout Griffin's personal and professional travels, it was a bold adventure, one of many that would continue to influence his interests and career while filling volumes of tales . . .

"My first trip to Europe was in 1932, when I was young, single and into the artist bit. I bought a round-trip ticket, third class, on a North German Lloyd steamer for $96.00, which included train fare from Boston to New York. Arrived in France, I bought a second-hand bicycle for a few dollars, and a Brittany fisherman's red outfit, with a beret. I bought a loaf of bread and a bottle of wine and took off. On my knapsack, between the handle-bars, I hung a metal sign saying "Repeal the 18th Amendment," a timely slogan in those days. It got lots of laughs in Paris and elsewhere.

"I actually traveled for a dollar a day in Europe, for this was still the depression era. In Rome I had a big room with a high ceiling in an old marble palace. Three meals a day for $8.00 a week . . . and even a bell over the bed to ring for breakfast. The same in Florence.

"One of my brightest memories involves one of those public urinals which always impress American travelers. At a French railroad station the train I was riding stopped just across the way from one of these conveniences. I was standing in the train passageway, leaning over the brass rail, when a Frenchman with more than adequate equipment uncovered himself in the urinal, in plain sight. Beside me stood some American college girls. Ignoring me, a supposed foreigner, they discussed the Frenchman's physique freely. As the train pulled away from the scene, I asked them meekly, in my best Boston English, 'Can you tell me what time it is?' They fled.

" *I took a camera along to shoot pictures I didn't have time to draw. Then I figured when I got home I could draw from the prints. After a little concentration with the camera, the old pen and ink seemed like a darn slow way to get something down on paper.*"

"Love It or Leave It: Advice of ace color man"
Graphic Graflex News
March, 1949

Sketch of Arthur Griffin,
France, 1932

"I was staying for a week in a fishing village in Brittany and a Russian artist noticed my hands as I was eating crusty French bread at the long dining table shared by all the boarders. She asked if I would pose for her. She would not give me the sketch so I photographed it."

In his travels, Griffin never made any attempt to learn the language of the country he was in. He believed that with his stutter, it would be worse than useless. He carried a dictionary in which, when necessary, he would point out words. In one Italian city, the mosquitoes in his bedroom were so tormenting he went to buy cheesecloth. The dictionary had no word for cheesecloth. In desperation (and fun), Griffin bought a lump of cheese, brought it to the drapier and laid it on a piece of cloth. Amidst a burst of laughter from the drapier and his customers, Griffin got his cheesecloth that became part of many other tales . . .

"In Italy, it was the Mussolini era when trains ran on time and guide books welcomed tourists to all hotels and dirt-cheap boarding houses. The least expensive places, the kind I stayed in, had no screens and the mosquitoes were a plague. Following the custom of the country, I bought myself a few yards of cheesecloth and nightly slept under a cheesecloth 'tent.'

"Another catch in Il Duce's paradise was registration. Hotel guests had to fill out a card at check-in that had to be in the local police station before midnight. Mussolini wanted to know all about everybody. A desk clerk usually helped me fill out the form. This worked until I got off the beaten track in Orvieto, a hill town, reached by a funicular railway, which I found late one night, tired and hungry.

"At the hotel desk the clerk shoved the card at me. I couldn't read it and the clerk couldn't explain it. So I just wrote whatever came into my head. Then I had a swell meal, washed down with lots of their famous free wine. I went to my room, rigged a cheesecloth tent and slept. The next thing I knew there was a banging on the door. I came to and tried to untangle myself from the cloth — I had no pajamas — as three of Mussolini's cops, with swords and three-cornered hats, burst into the room. I stood there and laughed. It turned out that from the way I had filled out my card, and from the clerk's description of me, the cops thought I was a miscreant they wanted."

France, 1932, Bromoil print

The Bromoil Print

The photographs taken during Griffin's 1932 trip became the cornerstone for his experiments with bromoil prints, a technique for integrating oil painting and photography. The bromoil print is a wonderful example of fine art photography from the "pictorialist" period . . . soft, painterly and romantic. Griffin, the artist, chose the bromoil print process at a time when photographers often tried to make their photographs, through inventive printing techniques, look as much like paintings as possible.

The following brief description of the process comes from Griffin's recollection and a photography book published in 1924. A photograph is placed in a bleaching and tanning solution that removes the visible image while hardening the gelatin base and creating a matrix. Although the image is no longer clearly evident, in a certain light one can see and feel the "relief," thick in areas of shadow and thin in highlighted areas. The paper, while still wet, is placed on a board, face up, and all excess moisture is removed. Oil paints, of any color, are then dabbed onto the paper, entirely covering its surface. Hundreds of quick, gentle, down/up strokes of a strong bristle brush, made for this work, pick up the ink from certain areas while more ink is applied in other areas. This stroking is done repeatedly and quickly until the image appears with the tonalities and contrasts sought by the artist. Paint is absorbed by the shadow and middle tone portions of the gelatin but not the highlight portions. Saturation and contrast are built by repeated applications. To create or deepen the highlights, an eraser is used to rub away more oil paint and add final touches. For Griffin, the process stopped here. However, another step for some artists is to transfer the treated image to a high quality paper to form another permanent print and image. Each print is original and, in Griffin's case, each is unique, a one of a kind vintage print.

The Griffin Bromoil Collection consists of about 24 prints from Europe and New England. It is but a small part of the wonderful pictures shot by Griffin as he traveled through Europe in '32. Following are examples of the Europe bromoils, vintage prints and a few never-before-seen 1932 photographs (New prints), all chosen for their clear influence and place in Griffin's career as a photojournalist and landscape photographer.

France, 1932, Bromoil print

France, 1932, New print

France, 1932, Bromoil print

France, 1932, Bromoil print

Italy, 1932, Bromoil print

Italy, 1932, New print

Top: *Holland, 1932, Vintage photograph*
Bottom: *Holland, 1932, New Print*

Germany, 1932, Bromoil print

Holland, 1932, Vintage photograph

THE *GLOBE* YEARS

Arthur Griffin worked at *The Boston Globe* from 1929 to 1946 when there was no more exciting place to be in the city of Boston, day or night. This was Newspaper Row, a two hundred yard stretch of Washington Street that was home to Boston's three major newspapers, the *Globe*, the *Post*, the *Transcript* and the offices of the Associated Press and the United Press among others. The *Globe* functioned in three buildings amidst a rabbit-warren of passage ways, crooked corridors, crowded rooms, and presses in the basement.

This was also a time of significant transition for the newspaper business, when photography and journalism merged and photojournalism was launched. Photography was playing an ever increasing role in the production of newspapers and rotogravure was becoming more popular. The rotogravure process made for better reproduction of photographs than the photoengraving process used for the reproduction of photographs. Yet it remained impractical until a paper's circulation went over 100,000.

In 1935, with a mass circulation of more than 100,000 and the accessibility of the high speed, high definition press, the *Globe* was ready for its first rotogravure . . . and so was Griffin. Jimmie Krigman, a fastidious co-worker senior to Arthur in the art department, was put in charge and asked Arthur to join him. Griffin was to design the layouts of the roto's pages, displaying the various photographs selected by Krigman.

Griffin decided not only to design layouts but to try his hand at photographs as well. From the relative isolation of artistic creation, of interminable draughtsmanship, Griffin was suddenly thrown into the rough-and-tumble competition of journalism. The *Globe*'s Rotogravure section was in competition with the best that the Hearst organization could offer. Taking the new position was risky and demanding. The pictures required photographic skill and the "big picture story," to which Arthur aspired, demanded inventiveness, foresight and imagination.

"You couldn't say I went into photography with the idea of making a living. I just drifted into it. I spent more and more time turning out prints instead of drawings in those early days, but I hung on to my commercial artist's work until I was sure I had a good thing going."

Love It or Leave It: Advice of ace color man."
Graphic Graflex News, *March 1949*

Griffin, to far left, with two 35mm cameras; other cameramen all still working with large format news cameras.

Over a three year period, "Griff" made his mark as one of New England's first "cameramen" and photojournalists. He was the first to work exclusively with the new 35 millimeter camera, a German Contax he could ill afford to buy. All the news photographers of the day used a large box camera with a bellows, called a Speed Graphic. Compared with the 35mm, it was cumbersome to hold, heavy to carry and slow, as it required a change of plate or "film" for every two pictures. News cameramen preferred the Graphic for speed of production. With a deadline hanging over him, a photographer had only to develop the one film. With the 35mm, the photographer had to develop the roll, select the negatives and then print, all requiring more time. The rotogravure, however, was published only once a week. Speed of production was not the prime consideration. Quality of image was. The 35mm camera permitted Griffin to take multiple pictures quickly, preserve the best and discard the worst.

Color photography was also available before the printing press was ready to present it to mass audiences. But the presses soon caught up and, on December 8, 1940, the first color picture to run in a Boston newspaper appeared in the *Boston Globe* . . . Griff's shot of Charles (Chucking Charlie) O'Rourke, quarterback for a spectacular Boston College team that had just tasted victory over Tulane University in the Sugar Bowl. The shot was taken with a 4″ × 5″ which Griffin reserved for most color work.

From 1935 to 1946, "Griff's" photographs, "firsts" and feature stories appeared almost weekly on the *Globe*'s Sunday Rotogravure covers and double spreads. He authored stories on "unknowns" such as architect Royal Barry Wills, scientist Dr. Edwin H. Land, and other New Englanders who would become forces in their own field. He documented the "first" and the "last" events, the "new" and the "old" and the "eternal." In black and white and in color, Griffin captured the essence of Boston and New England, her people and heroes, streets and landmarks, culture and commerce, natural disasters and war years, her work and leisure, and of course her weather. During his *Globe* years, his antics, experiences and stories became as legendary as his photographs . . .

1938

How This Cover Was Made

"With the smaller size of the 35mm camera and the ability to take many photos without having to reload film, I could take many candid shots of my subjects without distracting them from whatever they were doing. I would then print separate pictures, mount them on a board, and use black ink on the edges and background to complete what would appear in the *Globe* to be a single picture. The "action" candids are notable as fifty years ago, at the time these were made, only very slow speed film was available."

Presenting "The Next Mayor," October 31, 1937

In 1937 an unknown photographer caught Arthur Griffin in the act of persuading a very busy Mayor James Michael Curley, a famous and controversial Boston politician, to pose for a Globe *cover.*

The rotogravure cover of Boston's mayoral portraits was complete except for Curley who had, up to this time, not been cooperative. Griff had only one day left and, knowing Curley was on trial, he headed for the Court House. As Curley emerged Griff jumped along side of him. "Say now. You haven't been returning my calls and I've run out of time. I have new pictures of all the mayoral candidates except you. If you can't pose for me in the next hour, you'll have to forget being on the special cover." So persuasive was Griffin that Curley agreed to meet him at Boston's Parker House. Upon Griffin's arrival, an impatient and indignant Curley demanded to know what he should do. "Do what you do best. Speak." Curley, noted as a great orator, removed his coat and began. "These damn newspapermen. They take up my time. Cause problems . . . (how am I doing?) . . ." "Fine, keep going," replied Griff. Fifteen minutes later, he had his photos, his story, and his cover.

Fire! October 4, 1936

One "big picture story" Griffin planned was a panorama of fire engines emerging simultaneously from the eight bays of the new fire station on Bowdoin Square in downtown Boston. The preparation required the assistance of the police department to hold up traffic and the fire department to get all the equipment moving at the same time. Griffin had determined the best shooting location to be across the street on the second-floor fire escape at the local pool hall.

"As I was walking along the grating, I didn't see a hole in the grating where an iron ladder went down two stories to the street. I stepped into the hole. Fortunately, the camera was on a strap around my neck. I grabbed at one side or another as I fell, catching nothing, but those wild gestures kept me upright so that I somehow landed on my feet.

"Hundreds of spectators had been watching me and firemen raced across the street to help me. They were insisting on taking me to the Haymarket Relief Station, a clinic long since demolished. I talked them into letting me, battered and bleeding, go back upstairs to make my shots of the engines coming out of the bays. They did. The eight pieces of apparatus emerged together. I got my shots. Police let the traffic resume and firemen took me to the hospital where a doctor bandaged my head and my leg and took eight stitches in my hands. The worst damage was to my trousers. They were in shreds. We then continued to Boston Harbor where I, bandaged and disheveled, completed the story with a few photographs of the Harbor's finest fire-fighting boats."

Lee Griffin, daughter of Arthur and Claire, begins her design career early on a fall pumpkin, 1938.

Neighbor Bill Dingwell escorts a friend to school, 1940.

Boston's Monuments, 1937

Arthur at work . . . and play, 1937

"Boston, largest fishing port in the Western hemisphere," 1937

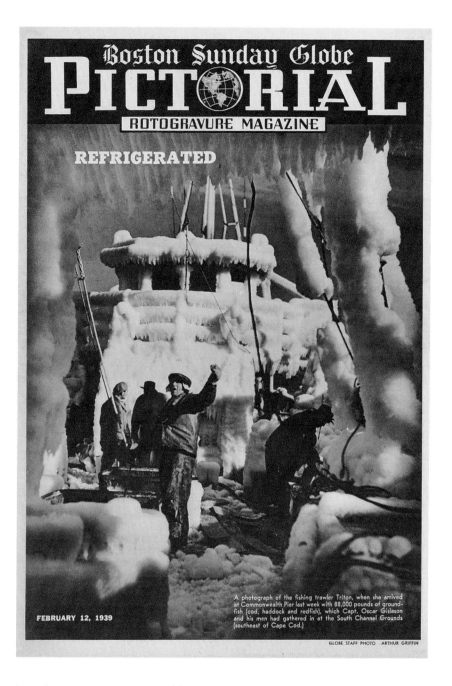

Trawler Triton, Commonwealth Pier, Boston, 1939

A 56-Year Wait, 1940

Cyrus E. Dallin, 22 years old, an obscure young student of sculpture from Utah, entered a contest 56 years ago for an equestrian statue of Paul Revere, to stand in Boston. Noted sculptors competed: Daniel Chester French, who did "The Minute Man," Thomas Ball who did the George Washington statue on the Public Garden, and others. But the unknown boy from the West won the award of a distinguished committee. The city was to put up $5000 and another $25,000 was to be raised from the public by the committee.

But criticism of the award to the unknown youth undermined the project. It collapsed. Cyrus Dallin became a great sculptor. His "Appeal to the Great Spirit" stands before the Boston Art Museum, one of the striking statues in the city. At seventy-nine, Dallin had his rejected statue accepted by the George Robert White Fund trustees, whose appropriation of $27,500 has paid for its execution in bronze, one and one-half times life size. Cast at the foundry of T.F. McGann in Somerville, it will be dedicated next Sunday on a pedestal of Milford pink granite on Paul Revere Mall, North End.

It stands against the background of the Old North Church, immortalized by Longfellow's poem of Revere's ride, as shown in the preview on the cover of this rotogravure.

Boston Globe *Rotogravure, September 15, 1940*

The Dallin story was perfect for Griffin's inventiveness and humor. As the city of Boston waited for the unveiling of Dallin's long-awaited Paul Revere, Griffin went into action. "In 1940 *The Boston Globe*'s Rotogravure was designed and laid out in Boston but printed in New York. It took three weeks to get anything in the 'Roto' and by then the news was stale. I wanted to 'beat the clock' and have a picture of the new statue on the cover a week before the unveiling. First I made a picture of the granite pedestal with a few kids standing at the base looking up to where the statue would be. Then I went to the McCann Foundry in Somerville and carefully took a picture of the statue as it would appear when placed on the pedestal. I made a large enlargement of the pedestal picture with the kids, and an appropriately scaled enlargement of the statue, and combined them to have a perhaps 'premature' but nevertheless fun scoop for the Roto cover."

Park Street Church

The Park Street Church and the Boston Common have over the years witnessed many significant events in Boston's history. Arthur Griffin, in the shadow of the magnificent Park Street spire, was witness to two very personal events.

"I stutter and I'm not sensitive about it. Once, however, I nearly got my head knocked off for it. One day I was making pictures on the Boston Common, near the Park Street Church. A very pretty young woman came up and asked me 'C-c-could you p-p-please tell me how to get to the P-p-public Garden?' I started to try and tell her. The next thing I knew she hauled off and hit me. A cop nearby came over and asked if I was bothering her. Before she could answer I yelled, 'This g-g-g-gal seems to think that s-s-s-she's the only p-p-p-person that s-s-s-stutters in all of B-b-b-Boston.'"

During World War II, the first blackout trial in Boston resulted in the following incident. "The night of the trial blackout I grabbed my Ikomat B and groped my way over to Boston Common for what turned out to be a night of many trials. First I tripped over a low wire and smashed my camera. I returned to my office, grabbed my Contax then carefully made my way back to the Common, near the State House. Just as I got ready for a shot, a cop approached and stopped me. I tried to explain that I had a permit—that the State Committee of Public Safety had given its okay to the press, but the cop hadn't been informed. Finally he disappeared into the darkness and I snapped my first shot. As I was changing the bulb, still somewhat blinded from its flash, a drunken man and woman pitched into me, the woman kicking and screaming, the man swinging and yelling that no one should take photos during a blackout. They grabbed my camera and ran off in the darkness just as another cop appeared and arrested me. Another cop took off after the 'patriotic' couple. We were all marched to the police station where I convinced the captain that I was within my rights to take pictures. My evening's work resulted in a sprained neck, bruised knee, smashed camera . . . and no pictures. And luckily no mug shot either."

"The Valentine Day Snowstorm that hit Boston in 1940 closed down the city and all surrounding communities for a long time. There was no way to get to Boston from Winchester where I lived. No cars or busses were running. Few roads were plowed. So I skied from Winchester, a distance of about 15 miles. I had a field day all over town. And got some great shots. As I was heading towards the State House, I spotted a couple skiing up Park Street, looking as though they were on their way to work. I got that shot, and many others. But that was the photograph that won me an award from the Boston Press Photographers' Association for 'best picture of the year.' As I said in a *Globe* article in 1943, 'You can't be told where and how to take prize winning pictures. You are likely to stumble upon them in the most unexpected places.'"

Globe *Photographer Wins Award — Mayor Maurice Tobin presents award for best feature picture of the year to Arthur Griffin of* The Boston Globe *staff for "Park Street Skiers."*

"Park Street Skiers," 1940

Valentine Day Snowstorm, 1940

Beacon Hill
SKI-TRAIL

By MARJORIE WATTS

Beacon Hill's many ski-minded residents found paradise right at their doorstep after Boston's St. Valentine Day blizzard of 1940—the worst since 1898. The gentle parallel slopes of Mt. Vernon and Chestnut sts.—even Myrtle's familiar length — became White Mountain slopes for the day, complete to the last atmospheric mitten.

AN INGENIOUS CAP and mittens right out of the Tyrol keep pretty Blake Schoenfuss of Louisburg Square warm, but her skiing trail begins at the State House.

TRAFFIC JAM on Mt. Vernon st. finds Elizabeth "Sister" Sears (right) and a number of the Sears' neighbors enjoying Winter sports in their front dooryards.

SUB-DEBUTANTES Julia Deane (left) of West Hill place and Alice Hunsaker of Louisburg Square find Beacon Hill a veritable Tuckerman's Ravine.

FASTEST METHOD OF TRAVEL over famous Beacon Hill is by skis and competent post-deb Frances McElwain (left) guides a party down Mt. Vernon st.

GLOBE STAFF PHOTOS, ARTHUR GRIFFIN

Beacon Hill Ski Trail, 1940

Dad Joins the Navy, August 9, 1942

"*The* Globe *helps to get recruits for the Navy from every part of the United States these days. It's all due to one of those extraordinary photographs taken by Arthur Griffin, the* Globe's *Sunday Rotogravure art camera man.*

Arthur went over to the Boston Navy Recruiting Station in the Post Office Building one day last summer. He saw Patrick J. Barry of Lynn sitting there waiting for a chance to enlist. The unusual part about Mr. Barry sitting there was that he wasn't alone — he'd brought his whole family with him, attractive Mrs. Barry, Junior and daughter Ann.

Arthur spotted the pictorial possibilities right away. It made a grand picture and a swell front page for the Globe's *Pictorial Section of last August 9. And, as far as Arthur was concerned, that was enough. But the men in the Recruiting Station's publicity division thought otherwise. They forwarded the Pictorial Section to headquarters in Washington.*

The men in Washington know a good thing when they see it, so they decided to use Arthur's front page shot for national recruiting purposes. They printed it in the September 19 issue of The Navy Recruiter, *the Navy paper through which recruiting stations throughout the country exchange ideas which help make ours a bigger and better Navy. The pulling-power of that photo shows up just as well in the* Recruiter, *through which it is made available to stations in 'mat' form. Last word was that the 'mats' (posters) were much in demand. (Hope there's enough to go around.)*"

Boston Globe Rotogravure, 1942

Spirit of '42

The famous painting, "The Spirit of '76," has hung in Abbot Hall in Marblehead, Massachusetts since the late 1800s. Painted by Archibald Willard, an unknown painter at the time, it was purchased for the town by General John H. Devereux of Ohio. Devereux believed that Marblehead, his birthplace, should have the painting that carried the spirit of America's colonial and revolutionary times and that, in the words of a writer of the time, "stirred the heart of a nation." The painting was Griff's inspiration for a roto cover. He first obtained permission to photograph "The Spirit of '76," then three soldiers from Fort Devens whom he positioned to resemble the militia men in the painting. With careful enlarging and printing he combined the two images into one picture for this unusual roto cover.

Boston's Big Guns Roar Defiance

By Gene R. Casey

TWO GENERALS watched proudly the other day, when, for the first time in nearly a generation, the big 12-inch guns of the Boston Harbor defenses spoke at Fort Warren. The 33-man crews of the best battery of the best battalion of the best National Guard Coast Artillery Regiment in New England were manning the guns. Battery A's crack gun crews, stripped to the waist, were jamming home 870 and 1070-pound shells and 275 pounds of powder at a time. They were firing at targets 10 miles away (they can fire 20 miles) and dropping shells where they wanted to so consistently that the Generals had good reason to be proud. This was the Generals' prize outfit, part of the first-place-winning 241st Regiment. These were the men on whom they must depend to protect Boston from ocean attack.

THE BIG 12 speaks with an authoritative voice in a flame-lit cloud of smoke. In foreground another crew gets ready to fire.

GLOBE STAFF ARTHUR GRIFFIN

FINAL CHECK. Battery A's commander, Capt. Edward B. Gallant, okays the giant rifle's readiness to blast its target.

LIEUT. COL. CHARLES W. BORDEN, ex-Medford High teacher, figures range of target.

LEADERS OF NEW ENGLAND'S BEST. Lieut. Col. Raymond A. Brocklehurst (right), acting commander of the 241st Coast Artillery Regiment, picked as best of Yankeeland's defenders; and Lieut. Col. Sarkis Zartarian, commander of the 241st's 1st Battalion, top battalion of the regiment.

TWO GENIAL GENERALS. Maj. Gen. Thomas A. Terry and Brig. Gen. Kenneth T. Blood, commanders, respectively, of the 1st Coast Artillery District and Boston Harbor Defenses.

HARD, brown bodies pressed on the ramrod, drive the shell home. (Lieut. Edwin R. Deagle supervises from atop the gun.)

Soap and water on the swab to keep that barrel spotless.

A kiss for Hitler from the boys' best gals. (The Fuehrer's name is scribbled on the shell.)

Boston's Big Guns Roar Defiance, August 24, 1941

"During World War II, all the armed services frequently approached the *Globe* to get pictures into the Roto for PR and recruitment. The Colonel of the Boston Harbor Defenses had promised to call me when the guns at Fort Warren were to be fired — the first time since World War I. And he did, but with the message that they were to go off in an hour. I was furious and said 'How can I possibly get out there in an hour?' He didn't care and said as much. Just at that moment Edward Rowe Snow, naval historian and story teller walked into my office. When I told him what had just occurred he said 'Arthur, meet me at Deer Island (Winthrop) and I'll have a boat for you.'

I tore off in time to catch a boat and arrive at Fort Warren as the guns were about to roar. When the commanding officer saw me he said 'Hey, you can't take any pictures' but, just as vehemently, I reminded him of his promise and phone call. He had to back-down. I got exclusive photographs and the *Globe* readers got a great, and exclusive story. Later that evening my family was having dinner. My mother-in-law was visiting. Suddenly she turned to me and asked why I was speaking so loudly. I had forgotten to remove the cotton from my ears stuck there just before the roar of Fort Warren's guns."

Boston Sunday Globe
PICTORIAL
JUNE 7, 1942

PHOTO BY ARTHUR GRIFFIN

A PLOWSHARE
for a PLANE

THE DAY the drive opened for farm scrap iron Nicholas Tedesco, whose farm is on the Ayer-Groton line, was one of the first farmers to bring his "country iron" to the scrap pile at Ayer. Tedesco had gathered 856 pounds of metal, including this old plowshare.
—*Story on Page 4*

1942

Boston Sunday Globe
PICTORIAL
APRIL 18, 1943

Globe Staff Photo Arthur Griffin

Spring Comes to Copley Sq.

The triangle in front of Trinity Church gives up its green sward for a Victory Garden. *See Page 3*

1943

Daughter of famous artist Thomas Hart Benton on Martha's Vineyard Beach, 1942

Young people of South Boston on piling alongside the old Dover Street bridge, 1942

THE BOSTON BOOK

Section I

Boston in Black and White

Over the years, Arthur Griffin had pestered Houghton Mifflin Company, Boston's oldest and leading publishing house, to publish a book of his color photographs. The answer was almost constant: "the photographs are marvelous but color printing is too expensive". At last, in 1946, Houghton Mifflin agreed to a book and suggested one of 114 photographs of Boston, only fourteen of which would be in color. The text was to be written by Esther Forbes, author of six novels about life in early New England and, in 1943, recipient of the Pulitzer Prize in history for *Paul Revere and the Times He Lived In.*

Although Griffin's photographs in the rotogravure had often carried a by-line, and his magazine work had already attracted national and international attention, his name was not widely known among the New England book reading public. That of Miss Forbes was. Born in Westborough, Massachusetts, a small town in the middle of the state, she had been educated at Bradford Academy and the University of Wisconsin. She had worked for Houghton Mifflin from 1920 to 1927 when she married and left publishing to write. With her wide reader recognition and familiarity with Boston, she was a good choice to collaborate with Griffin on *The Boston Book.*

Over dinner at the Griffins' home, the two collaborators discussed what Boston landmarks should appear in the book. Sitting on the floor, Miss Forbes recited the names of parks and neighborhoods, buildings and cemeteries, historic facades and sculpture, while Griffin produced hundreds of color transparencies and black and white photographs, some taken while on *Globe* assignments. When they were through, they found that he needed to take only two additional photographs to complete their list. These he was able to get the next day on his way to work at the *Globe.*

"She was wonderful to work with," Griffin said of Forbes, "gracious and very generous." Already established in her own field, she asked that Arthur Griffin's name appear first on the book and gave him the lion's share of the royalties. As a young photographer, still making his mark professionally, Griffin recognized the value and generosity of her suggestion.

Reviews were consistently flattering. Newspapers carried a picture of Griffin, Forbes, Temporary Mayor Hynes and Michael T. Kelleher, President of the Boston Chamber of Commerce. The publicity and the book proved a heady experience and brought Griffin's name and talent before a new audience.

"I had fun and exercise getting these photographs of Boston, and I also had to do quite a bit of advance planning to picture the subjects in the best and most dynamic way. Most buildings are not very photogenic or interesting unless you can get unusual lighting, frame the picture effectively, or get personalities in the scene. Telephoto and wide angle lenses, different filters, flash combined with sunlight can transform a mediocre subject into an exciting one . . . . You can't get the best angles and views by always staying on the ground. I took some of the pictures from a plane . . . . To get the grasshopper on top of the cupola of Faneuil Hall, I had to climb countless stairs and ladders, open a skylight, and trust a muscular janitor to hold my legs while I leaned out and shot skyward."

The Boston Book, *1947*

In Section I, all photographs are taken from *The Boston Book*, published in 1947. Together Griffin and Forbes "give the stranger and the native a picture of Boston that few can match."

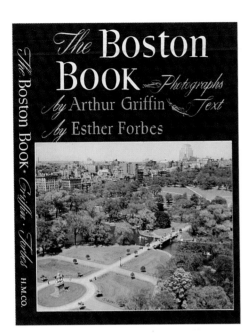

"Nature intended Boston to be a seven hundred acre peninsula of rocks, hills, gravel, and salt marsh, stretching out into Boston Harbor like a clenched fist. By now most of Boston is made land. Wherever in Boston you find yourself upon a hill and the streets crooked and narrow, you are in the original city. Like most large American cities, Boston has far outgrown its original swaddling clothes . . . . The pictures . . . have been largely taken from within the limits of the earlier city.

"Probably no city in America has furnished more jokes — its banned books, and its uplift, its baked beans, rubber plants, sensible shoes, brown bread, codfish cakes, and accent, the markers on the trees in the Public Garden (so one may improve the mind even as one enjoys the shade), the mudscrapers, serious culture, and traffic snarls. It is even considered a little slow . . . . But no American city has been more loved. The gold dome of the State House and the lavender panes on Beacon Hill . . . . The vitality of the waterfront . . . . Children screaming for joy in the Frog Pond, sailors afloat in swan boats, the exquisite rise of a church spire, the music of Symphony, the treasures of its museums, and the activities of generations of scholars. Boston can still mix idealism with indifference — and be called hypocritical. And still, for better or worse, walks a little by her wild lone." *Esther Forbes*

Right Top: *Old King's Chapel*
New England's first Episcopal Church, established in 1688 and erected some 50 years later, became, after the Revolution, the first Unitarian Church in America. It was in colonial times "a royal pet. Queen Anne gave it red cushions and vestments, James II its present pulpit, George III its communion plate. Handel helped procure its organ." Esther Forbes
Right Bottom: *"Around the corner in Court Street is the famous steaming kettle above the sidewalk which advertises another coffee stall . . . Boston is one of the few remaining cities where old-time artisans and tradesmen still proclaim their crafts with representative street signs." Lucius Beebe*

Left: *Old State House*
Right: *Old State House, Gracious Interior. Built in 1713, the Old State House was the center of business until 1795 when the new State House was erected. James Otis made his famous last speech in its council room, a speech of which John Adams said, "then and there independence was born."*

Above: *The Faneuil Hall weathervane, a glass-eyed copper grasshopper, has been trying to keep its eye on Boston's weather for over two hundred and fifty years.*

Left: *Dock Square and Faneuil Hall, "The Cradle of Liberty"*
From the seventeenth century to today, this has been a lively and picturesque market area for resident, visitor, vendor and tradesman. The original hall was given to Boston by Peter Faneuil, a successful immigrant and merchant, to be used as a market below and a meeting center above. It is from the public meetings, above and below, that it gained the name "Cradle of Liberty."

Above left: *Beyond Cyrus Dallin's statue of Paul Revere is Christ Church, The Old North Church of Longfellow's poem. The oldest church building in Boston (1732), its interior has been little changed through the years though its spire is 16 feet shorter than in the time of Paul Revere.*
Above center: *The present Custom House Tower stands at the head of what was the original Long Wharf.*
Above right: *Quincy Market. Back of Faneuil hall is Quincy Market, the greatest monument built by Josiah Quincy, one of Boston's first and great mayors. Built in 1826, it has been a center for commerce, visitors and performing street artists.*

Left: *Sam Adams, "a statesman incorruptible and fearless," with The Custom House Tower to the right.*

Above: *Boston seen from across the water toward the end of a summer day.*
Left: *Once the largest ships in the world tied up along T Wharf.*
Below: *Boston has always been considered an important port but enjoyed for many years the reputation as the greatest fish port in the world and the second most important port for transatlantic travel.*

Above: *The new Boston State House and Brewer Statue*
In 1795, Charles Bullfinch, at the age of 24, was asked to design a new center of government for Boston. His design, set on Beacon Hill, the highest hill in Boston, in Esther Forbes' words "nobly expressed the aspirations of his young country." Its normally gilded dome has remained one of the city's most famous landmarks, even during World War II when it was painted grey.

Below: *During the time of architect Bullfinch, much of Beacon Hill was removed, and the Hill's present streets and homes constructed. Parallel to*

Beacon Street ("The sunny street which holds the sifted few." Oliver Wendell Holmes) is Chestnut Street where one still finds lavender panes of glass. Next over from Chestnut Street is Mount Vernon. Henry James said it was "the only respectable street in America," but in Puritan days it was known as Mount Whoredom.

The Shell
"Along the Charles River runs the 'Esplanade,' a grassy parkway, stretching for two miles. It is lovely in summer with the sea breeze shipping in off the sea, the little sailing boats, racing shells, children playing, gulls screaming. And it is lovely in winter with black ice, skaters, and a frosting of white snow. Across the Charles in Cambridge are the domed buildings of M.I.T. The Esplanade is never more characteristic than on those hot summer nights when night after night thousands swarm about the Shell to listen to the concerts played by members of the Boston Symphony Orchestra." Esther Forbes

Left: *The Boston Public Library*

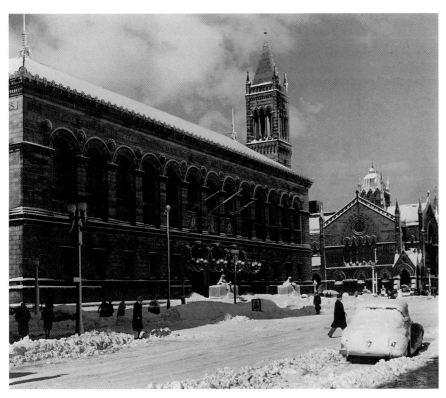

The Boston Public Library
Copley Square is home to the Boston Public Library, the picturesque "new"
Old South Church and the beautiful Trinity Church. The present library, built
in 1895 as a free library, was a rather new idea at the time.

*"In Boston they ask, 'How much does he know?' In New York, 'How much
is he worth?' In Philadelphia, 'Who were his parents?'"* Mark Twain

Museum of Fine Arts and Dallin's "Appeal to the Great Spirit"
The magnificent Museum of Fine Arts is located within an area long know
for its art, music, learning and baseball. It has been said for years that there
are more students in the Fens and within 25 miles of Boston than anywhere
else in the world.

The Christian Science Church
The Christian Science Church in Boston is 'The Mother Church' for all Christian Scientists. The original church, joined to the large domed modern building, contains a history of its founder, Mary Baker Eddy.

Section II

Boston in Color

Every city has its own color, the silvery sheen of Paris, the rich murkiness of London, the gray and white towers of New York, and the glaring whiteness of Miami. The memory of Boston is of a reddish or even rosy city. Above is a sky sometimes close and lowering, sometimes radiantly fresh, far away and blue, but always changing. About the city the sea changes with the sky. In the warm months, there is much green about Boston. In winter there is snow — white, dazzling, and so amazingly full of its own colors. It would be impossible to picture Boston merely with text and black and white. It is a city of color." *Esther Forbes*

For this section we have chosen to pair the color photographs taken by Griffin in the 1940s with shots taken by him, from the same locations, fifty years later in the early 1990s. It is still a city of color.

Commercial Wharf
Note on the far right the "New" Court House and Boston's famous landmark, the Custom House Tower, to the left.

63

Boston's Public Garden and Swan Boats, Summer
Across the Boston Public Garden and Common one can see the gold dome of
the State House, painted gray during World War II.

Copley Square

Faneuil Hall

Boston's Public Garden and Skyline, Winter
Shot from the roof of The Ritz Carlton Hotel, one of
Griffin's favorite spots for photographing Boston.

Boston Skyline from the Charles River

Section III

Generations Yet to Come

"Down streets and . . . squares have passed generations of men and women, some good, some bad; most of them unrecorded and a few famous to this day. It is their city. It is our city and in part already belongs to the generations yet to come." *Esther Forbes*

Arthur Griffin has always loved Boston . . . her streets and landmarks, culture and commerce, and her people and heroes. His photographs and stories, that delighted thousands in the *Globe's* rotogravures, showed his love for people and his ability to capture their vitality, moods and moments in time . . . of and for all generations.

The excellence of this work was acknowledged not only with the publication of *The Boston Book* but also by an important exhibition of Griffin's work. Zeiss, a fine German camera company, impressed by Griffin's work, organized in 1939 an exhibition of 51 photographs taken with two Zeiss "miniature" cameras, the Contax and the Super Ikonta B. Publicity for the exhibition said "(Griffin and his cameras) have become a familiar team throughout New England covering a wide range of events in the field of news and features. Rotogravure was the medium that brought out the finesse and skill of Arthur Griffin. He worked for many years as an artist with brush and pen and the knack of composing good pictures soon became part of him."

We have chosen for this section only a few photographs from the Zeiss Collection that portray well Boston's "generations."

Young Boxer. Charlestown Boys Club

Cooling Off

The Park Bench Scholar

Strolling Shadows

PIONEER AND ENTREPRENEUR

Arthur Griffin's inventive mind and independent spirit, combined with a fine business acumen, has for 90 years, supported well his professional and personal journey. Griffin began his entrepreneurial days at the age of ten as a delivery boy for the local newspaper, the *Lawrence Tribune*. He created the route himself and built it to more than 100 customers. In time he expanded his business to include *The Boston Globe* and the *Boston Post*.

His days as a student at the New School of Design, supported in part by a newspaperboy scholarship, likewise reflected an entrepreneurial spirit. Most of his fellow students were World War I veterans and would get a check every two weeks. As a result there was often a game of craps in the men's toilet, and whenever he played, the Griffin luck ran well. He remembers vividly one day, the principal came in and looked directly at him. Arthur froze. At Lawrence High School he would have been expelled. The principal merely asked how he was doing.

Upon graduating from art school, Arthur found that business was plentiful and immediately went to work drawing pictures of lighting fixtures, from 8:00 a.m. to noon, for $5.00 a week and designing signs in the afternoon for $20.00 a week. He was allowed to pitch a cot on the premises of Mr. Brand's lighting fixture shop, use the telephone and list Brand's address as his headquarters for freelance art work. When the company moved to a new location, Arthur and his cot went with them.

His first *Globe* position in the art department, from 6:00 p.m. to 1:00 a.m., also gave him time to freelance for three major publishing companies in Boston: designing book jackets for Houghton Mifflin, layouts for *House Beautiful* and hand-lettered headings for the *National Sportsman*.

During Griffin's years with the *Globe* his photography caught the attention of editors of many publications. Chief among them was *Life* magazine beginning, in 1936, what was to be a glittering decade as the outstanding picture magazine of its time. In 1938 *Life* offered Griffin a job on their staff in New York but Griffin was reluctant to leave either the *Globe* or New England. With the blessing of the *Globe*, he became *Life*'s man in New England, working first on a retainer and later on a freelance basis. The *Globe* benefited as well. It would be able to use, without charge, any of the work Griffin did while on a *Life* assignment.

Over the next few years, Griffin began selling his photographs to a wide audience and market. He became New England photographer for *Time* as well as *Life* and was a frequent contributor to *Colliers*, *The Saturday Evening Post* and other regional, national and international magazines.

"Learn something about composition and color harmony. Get a job that keeps you in bread and highballs and go at color slowly and carefully. Prove your worth with black-and-whites. Then when you're ready, the chances are editors will know something about your black-and-white work, and you can cinch it with a good looking file of color you've accumulated. Once you've proven yourself the jobs come easy."

Love It or Leave It: Advice of ace color man."
Graphic Graflex News, *March 1949*

Increasingly he knew he wanted the freedom of the freelance photographer. Increasingly he knew he could do it. On an excursion to Vermont in 1944 with his wife and daughter, Griffin spent two days taking fifteen shots of the foliage and mountain scenery and sent them to *The Saturday Evening Post*. They immediately bought six which they used a year later in a two-page spread. The *Post* sent him a check for $750. At that time Griffin was making $75.00 a week at the *Globe*. Soon after, Houghton Mifflin Company, Boston's oldest and leading publishing house, signed a contract for Arthur's first book. It was indeed time to move on to a new life and, ultimately, to a new direction with his work. In 1946, Griffin left the *Globe* to work for himself.

Griffin's freelance status gave him the freedom to explore new professional domains. Ever looking to the future, he determined to learn all about color photography, still in its infancy. In 1946 he went to Eastman Kodak in Rochester, New York to study what was, at the time, the only available commercial color printing process. Dye transfer printing, perfected by Robert Speck and Louis Condax of Philadelphia in 1935, was finally introduced by Kodak to the commercial market in 1945. Griffin returned to Boston from Rochester well schooled and well connected to Kodak.

Although he had been experimenting with color for many years, it now became his life, the landscape his focus. His interest did not shift to photography as art. For him it was irrelevant. What he knew was that the technological advances in color printing were creating a demand for color photographs that had never existed before.

Once again Griffin's timing was perfect. Assignments poured in keeping him busier than he dreamed he could be. National, international and regional magazines called upon him for special assignments or made frequent use of his stock files: *Saturday Evening Post, Woman's Day* (when it was still only 2 cents a copy), *Coronet, Colliers, Holiday* (perhaps the finest international travel magazine of its time), *Country Gentleman*, and many others from throughout the United States and Europe.

Kodak called upon him for numerous ad campaigns and made good use of his growing New England stock files. His work continued to be used frequently by *The Boston Globe*. Magazine covers and stories, advertisements, annual reports, calendars, telephone book covers and finally award-winning color pictorial books of New England were all part of Griffin's many freelance activities and contributions to the field of commercial photography. Each leaves behind another Griffin tale . . .

Into a Quincy Quarry, August 8, 1938
During the 1930s and '40s, while Griffin was an accredited New England photographer for Life *magazine, two of his photographs — a candid of fiery congressman Joe Martin of Attleboro, Massachusetts, and a group of boys diving into a Quincy quarry swimming hole — became* Life *covers.*

Charles (Chucking Charlie) O'Rourke , December 8, 1940
First color used on a Globe cover.
Griffin, already using color film on his own, was asked by Davis Taylor, Publisher of the Globe, to "shoot" Chucking Charlie O'Rourke, a rather spindly quarterback for the outstanding Boston College team that had just won national attention with a victory over Tulane University in the Sugar Bowl. O'Rourke was a great football star who had been named by Grantland Rice, dean of American sportswriters, to his all-America team.

God Gave Them Plenty, November 18, 1945
Second Globe color cover
Until Kodak brought out Kodachrome color film in the late 1930s there was no practical method to reproduce full color photographs in newspapers. Even then it was expensive and difficult to print properly. As the new Kodachrome film was slow, cameras had to be installed on tripods and good action wasn't possible. Taken on a tripod with a 4″ × 5″ camera, all the "Pilgrims" in the picture had to hold their pose for several seconds.

They've Built 3000 Ships by Hand

SHIPYARD OF 1668

IN 1668 THE TOWN GRANTED THE ADJACENT ACRE OF LAND "TO THE INHABITANTS OF IPSWICH FOR A YARD TO BUILD VESSELS AND TO EMPLOY WORKMEN FOR THAT END". THE SHIPBUILDING INDUSTRY HAS CONTINUED UNINTERRUPTEDLY IN ESSEX SINCE THAT DATE.

MASSACHUSETTS BAY COLONY TERCENTENARY COMMISSION

UP near the northeastern corner of Massachusetts a slim stream of tidewater reaches in from the Atlantic to give the small town of Essex a big place in shipbuilding history. Here, for almost 300 years, wooden ships have been sliding into blue water, while generations of Essex craftsmen watched appreciatively.

Essex had passed its second century of shipbuilding before iron plates pushed oaken planks from most shipyards. Today, in this quiet town of 1500, men still build wooden ships mostly by hand, and they are proud of the fact that their yards have sent more than 3000 sturdy ships down to the sea since 1668. Nowadays, of course, there is some modern machinery in the three Essex shipyards still in operation. The whine of the power saw and the electric drill is mixed with the softer sound of planes and the dubbing adz. But most of the timbers are fitted by hand, and all, no matter how heavy, are lifted into place without benefit of power cranes.

The Julie Ann, a stubby-masted fishing boat, whose construction is pictured on these pages, is typical of Essex's current efforts. Not beautiful, but quite useful, this recent product of one Essex yard is 102 feet long, and is powered by a 350-horsepower Diesel engine. It was built in the Essex yard of Jonathan Story, whose family feels apologetic because its members have been building ships for only about 100 years.

Eighteen men spent ten months on this fishing boat, which, after being launched in the Essex River at high tide, had to be taken to Gloucester to be wired for electricity and fitted with its engine. Leo Favaloro, a Gloucester fisherman, paid $150,000 for the Julie Ann, but he should soon earn this money back, as the ship can bring 225,000 pounds of fish in to Eastern markets on each successful trip. Before starting this job, the Julie Ann, named for two of Leo's daughters, was blessed by a priest, then, with a full crew of merrymakers aboard, made a tour of Gloucester Harbor.

In Essex, meanwhile, other keels were being laid, other oaken frames steamed and bent to support newer ships. Viewed through the golden haze of accumulated years, the labors of Essex shipbuilders seem almost heroic. You might even be willing to believe the legend which claims that the first Essex ship was built in a garret, and that the house had to be torn apart to get it out. Yet today, along the salt marshes and mud flats of Essex where flat-bottomed dories cruise in search of clams, you will hear no loud praise of Essex shipbuilding. Instead there is the reserved New England admission, "Boats? Yes, we build a few here."

PHOTOGRAPHY BY ARTHUR GRIFFIN

Starting work on the "Julie Ann" these Essex craftsmen put together an oak frame. The wood pegs in the frame in left foreground are called "trunnels."

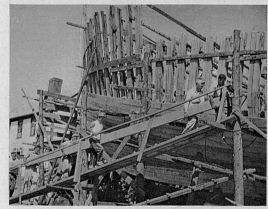
This heavy oak plank, carried by six men, became part of the "Julie Ann's" hull above the waterline; below the waterline hard-pine planks were used.

The almost completed ship collects a coat of paint, and some bright gilding on her name lettering. Soon afterward she made the trip to Gloucester.

You can count the "Julie Ann's" ribs at this stage of construction. When completed, she had 49, all jockeyed into place without benefit of power cranes.

Planks that must be bent are steamed in this box to make them more pliable. All timbers were cut right in Essex yards from slabs of oak and hard pine.

The solid hull, being calked by workmen, helps explain why Gloucester fishermen prefer Essex ships: they are heavier built, outlast even steel ships.

As is customary in Essex yards, work on the "Julie Ann" continued in all seasons. Snow and rain water, lying in the hull, helped to swell the planks.

Father Joseph Sullivan of Gloucester blesses the "Julie Ann," while Owner Leo Favaloro, second from his right, and relatives and friends stand by.

The finished product cruised Gloucester Harbor for one festive day, then went to work. She now carries a crew of 15 out on two-week fishing trips.

Opposite left: *"They've Built 3000 Ships by Hand," February 28, 1948*
The first color photographs in The Saturday Evening Post, *appearing in the*
fall of 1945, were by Arthur Griffin, a series of photographs of Vermont fall
foliage shot in 1944. Griffin was paid $750, ten times his weekly salary at the
time. Three years later they printed "3000 Ships" and ran the following story.

Inside Information: A Picture Story That Took a Year to Do

The Saturday Evening Post ran the following story in the same edition as
"3000 Ships."

Photographer Arthur Griffin had to display considerable agility last August in
completing two assignments during a single day: a christening in Massachusetts
and a wedding in Maine.

Griffin had been planning to photograph the christening for nearly a year
— an expected nine months had been prolonged by shortages of materials.
With the blessings of Post *editors, he had kept a colorful photographic record*
of each step leading up to the christening, which was to provide the final picture
in the series. Every few weeks he had driven from his home in Winchester,
Massachusetts, to Essex to record the progress of the Julie Ann, *a wooden fish-*
ing vessel whose embryonic history is told in the Post *picture story, "They've*
Built 3000 Ships by Hand."

"I'd had the step-by-step story in mind for several years," he says. "But
I knew that I would have to be around for eight or nine months to complete
the series — this ship took a year due to delays in getting proper timbers, and
so on — and was afraid that I'd have the set nearly completed when I'd get
an assignment that would keep me from finishing it."

He decided to try, anyhow, and talked the idea over with Photography
Editor Doug Borgstedt. The project was launched at about the same time
that the keel of the Julie Ann *was laid.*

"I found that I had plenty of leeway after starting the pictures," he
continues. "Most stages in the building lasted several weeks, so I could wait
for perfect photography weather before driving over to Essex. I had to visit
the ship at specific times only for the launching — it poured that day — and
the christening of the vessel in Gloucester harbor."

Griffin had already taken on a wedding-picture job for a Saturday
when he learned that the christening of the Julie Ann *would take place that*
same afternoon. The wedding was in Kennebunkport, some 75 miles from
Gloucester.

"I told the ship's owner that he'd just have to have the christening in the
morning," Griffin says. "Morning was a better time for the color photographs
anyhow. I made the pictures far out in the harbor, then the captain hailed a
passing fishing schooner which took me back to Gloucester."

Griffin arrived in Kennebunkport with 15 minutes to spare. The wedding,
incidentally, was that of Photography Editor Borgstedt.

The Face of AMERICA

Autumn Magic

The sorcerer waves his wand, changing colors at will, bringing the great illusion to a flaming climax. The haunting wind music mutes before the final crescendo, as the last performance of the season draws to a close. Soon the curtain will fall, and the theater of all outdoors—cold, drafty and draped in white—will stand empty for next spring's opening. Here in New England the first thin watery snowfall signals a warning, and the maple leaves of Sugar Hill, New Hampshire, in colorful costume still, hasten to make their exit, fluttering offstage as gracefully as ballerinas. The sorcerer bows, folds his dark cloak about him and departs. Icy winter has no pity for mountebanks such as he, and his next show doesn't begin until April. • Photograph by Arthur Griffin

Autumn Magic, November 3, 1956, The Saturday Evening Post
These double page color spreads were a weekly feature in the Post. *Griffin's work was frequently featured.*

The
Face
of
AMERICA

Geyser
on the
Green

When Boston's humid heat pushes
past the ninety mark, new
Bostonians bearing such unlikely
Yankee names as Spinazzola,
Murphy and Leonadakis gather
at the Frog Pond on the Common
to watch their children splash
and frolic, squealing in the fountain's
cooling water. Three hundred
years ago, when Governor John
Winthrop set aside the Common as
a "trayning field and pasture
for cattell," Frog Pond was a muddy,
shallow, spring-fed hole, its
surface flecked with skipped-stone
flashes and the silent rings
of blinking frogs. Today the pond
is changed as are the names
of Yankee youngsters playing in it.
It is a city substitute for the
Atlantic's brown salt sands too
far away for easy travel.
● Photograph by Arthur Griffin

Geyser on the Green, The Saturday Evening Post

Opposite page: *First color in* Yankee *Magazine,*
December, 1959
Stark, New Hampshire

Another photographic first were the color
spreads in Yankee *Magazine which helped*
confirm the high quality the public came to
expect from that publication. Arthur produced
twelve a year for four years. In later years,
these 48 photographs were to form the basis
of Griffin's book New England, *the first all*
color photographic book on New England.

The first color photograph Griffin sold to Eastman Kodak Company, 1948. (Last sale to them was in 1974.)

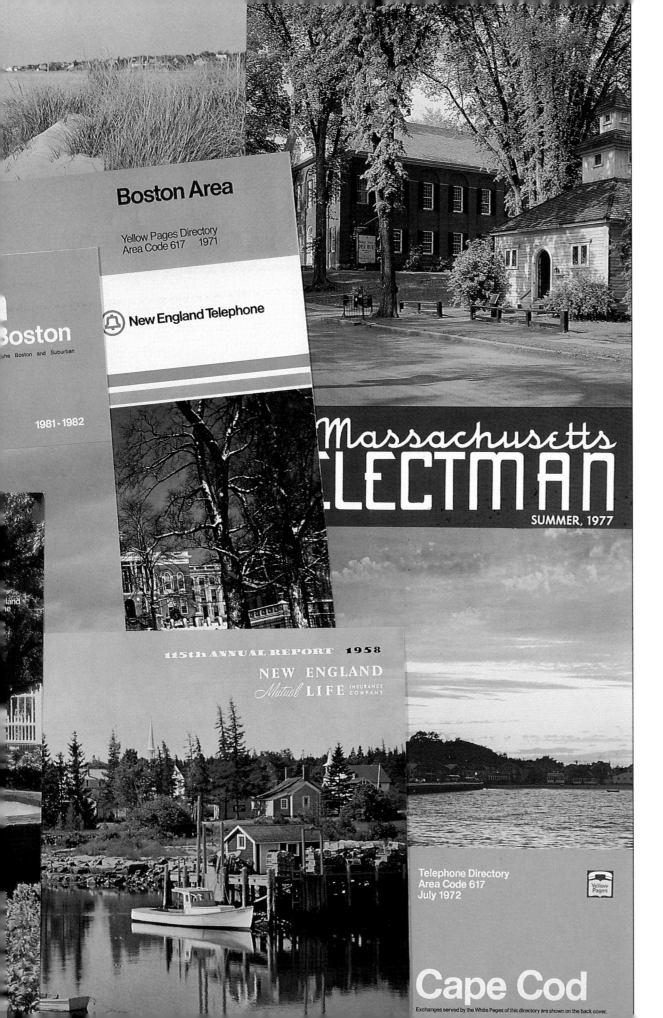

Friendships and contacts have always been important to Griffin. One was Elliston Bell, art director of the Yellow Pages at New England Telephone Company. As a young artist, Griffin designed many of the advertisements in the Yellow Pages. Eventually he went to Bell with the idea of putting his color photographs of New England on the covers of New England Telephone directories. Bell went for the idea. The first year Griffin's pictures appeared on their covers for all sections of New England. For many years, his photographs were enjoyed by the telephone company's public.

Another long and enjoyable relationship has existed between Arthur and the Massachusetts Municipal Association. For 15 years they have used four Griffin photographs a year for covers of their different publications. The relationship continues.

For 60 years Griffin has traveled New England's coastline and back roads shaping "the halcyon way we like to look at New England." It is a rare home that does not have an Arthur Griffin photograph from a telephone book, calendar, annual report, magazine, or book. Undoubtedly millions of people have enjoyed his photographs without knowing their source.

North
Suburban Boston
With Chelsea Area Yellow Pages

Localities served by the White Pages of the Boston and Suburban directories are shown on the back cover. See Page 1 of the Yellow Pages for the localities served by the Yellow Pages of this directory.

New England Telephone

Telephone Directory
Area Code 617
1977 - 1978

yellow pages

An Exceptional Work of Art

Two things can be said of art. First, that distortion is at the heart of it; and second, that luck is often a major factor in its creation, even though, in baseball parlance, the artist makes his own breaks. Both of these axioms relate to one of the most discussed photographs Arthur Griffin ever took. The occasion was sunset; the place was Horn Pond in Woburn, not far from his home; the season was Spring. Viewed horizontally, the picture is a splendid landscape. Turned on its side, it becomes a surrealist masterpiece.

Held sideways the picture presents a strange skeletal figure of a nude woman with a disproportionate head like a miniature watchtower . . . . The hips swell sensually; a spider sits at the navel; the swell of the breasts is suggested by a triangle of branch pointing upward toward the throat from which the shoulders slope in a feminine declension. The absence of arms does not detract from the force of the portrait . . .

Chosen for its serene landscape, the picture was put on the cover of a New England Telephone Company directory. The secret portrait (unobserved by Griffin) was discovered by the company's customers. Some were startled, some amused, a few offended, and someone called it "obscene." So many calls came in, the company had to prepare a stock reply. No one seemed to realize that photographic skill and an element of luck had produced a picture that can only be regarded as an exceptional work of art.

Herbert A. Kenny
Arthur Griffin's New England: The Four Seasons

Opposite page left: *William A. Robinson, boatbuilder and yachtsman*
Opposite page right: *One of Griffin's photographs from the trip became a* Boating *Magazine cover*

The Boudreau Fleet, Voyageur *and* Caribee, *St. Lucia, 1960*
The Griffins sailed on both, first off Cape Breton (left), then St. Lucia (right).

 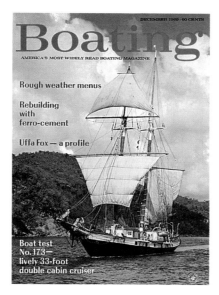

Just before the onset of World War II, Arthur was asked by the *American Magazine* to photograph William A. Robinson of Ipswich, Massachusetts, an avid nautical adventurer and ship builder. A young man, Robinson had built a fine shipyard on the Crane estate in Ipswich where he specialized in fishing vessels and cruising yachts adapted from old plans of clippers, brigantines and other early schooners. With the onset of the war his shipyard was converted to naval military purposes. Years later, the Griffins were invited to sail for several weeks in the West Indies with a Captain Boudreau, a war hero and expert seaman who operated a charter business in St. Lucia and on the Brad Dor Lakes of Cape Breton, Canada. The Griffins had first sailed with him, while on assignment with *The Saturday Evening Post,* off Cape Breton on a 96-foot schooner and had become good friends. In 1960, Boudreau expanded his business to St. Lucia where the Griffins sailed with him and, to their delight, found themselves on a schooner built 20 years earlier by shipwright Robinson of Ipswich.

Griffin's work for the Globe continued long after his 1946 decision to leave the Globe and pursue a career in freelance photography. As with much of his later work, he captured the New England landscape and seasons.

Griffin had an enjoyable arrangement with Libby•Owens•Ford Glass Company, begun when the President of the New England Chamber of Commerce, an old friend of Griffin's, personally brought Griffin's work to the attention of their advertising department. L•O•F asked him to photograph picturesque New England scenes through an automobile windshield made of L•O•F glass. (Arthur made sure it was standard equipment on his own station wagon).

Luck was with Arthur when he and Claire left home at 6:00 a.m. to photograph the Quoddy Lighthouse in Lubec, Maine. Located over 300 miles from Boston, the Lighthouse is almost on the Canadian border. Arthur had photographed the lighthouse many times and knew of a road that led to the only good location from which to photograph. In the afternoon the sun would be on the lighthouse. The day was overcast but as they drove down the gravel road the sun came out for the first and only time that day. Working quickly, they managed to get a few pictures before the sun disappeared. They spent the night in Lubec returning to the lighthouse the next morning. Again fog. The lighthouse keeper's wife met them with the tale that she had not been able to hang her laundry out to dry for over a week. It turned out to be one of those summers when the week of fog turned into months. But Arthur had his photo.

Top: *Peacham, Vermont, 1964*
Bottom: *Quoddy Lighthouse, Lubec, Maine, 1964*

Season's Greetings, 1958-'59

VISIT THE
Kodak
EXHIBIT

The World's Largest Color Transparency from the Kodak COLORAMA, Grand Central Station, New York, 1958–1959

During Griffin's 25-year association with Eastman Kodak Company, he was given a number of special assignments including the COLORAMA installed in New York City's Grand Central Station. Measuring 60 feet wide by 18 feet high, these photographs were changed every three weeks during a period of 30 years. The transparencies were mounted, with hundreds of lights behind them, high in the station above the bustling throng of hurrying commuters.

This shot, taken in 1958, has always been one of Arthur's favorites, perhaps for the story as much as the image. The only way he could capture this beautiful Peacham, Vermont scene was from the field but it was too flat, too empty. So Griffin hired the town highway department to plow a "road" across the snow-covered corn field and hired a red sleigh pulled by a black horse to come along the road. The maneuvering took time. No sooner had the road been plowed than the sun disappeared. It snowed and he had to arrange for a second plowing. Finally, with an obliging sun and with a touch of persistence, ingenuity, patience and luck, he had another New England classic. For three weeks, Griffin's image carried Season's Greetings, 1958– 1959, to all New York . . . and the world.

TED WILLIAMS

Ted Williams and Arthur Griffin met in an historic hour. It was 1939; Ted was about to seize the role of Rookie of the Year and Eastman Kodak had created a new color film they wanted Griffin to try. Griffin was at Fenway Park with his usual assortment of equipment, working on a story, in black and white, for the *Globe*. But he carried with him his 4″ × 5″ view camera and Kodak's new color film made specifically for the 4″ × 5″ cameras.

Williams agreed to pose. At that moment, all was propitious. Ted, who later became soured by his treatment at the hands of carping columnists, was amiable, relaxed, and even eager to be photographed. For two hours they worked together. Griffin worked mainly with his black and white equipment for his *Globe* story. The use of color in the *Globe* was still a year away. But he experimented, for himself and Kodak, with the color film.

The color film was slow, not good for action shots, but Williams, exhibiting his batting stance and his swing, was so engaging a figure, so handsome, so much the American hero, that Griffin was determined to shoot him in color as well as black and white. He noticed that at the end of Ted's swing, when the bat had slipped from the double grip and was still held only in the right hand now behind the batter, there was a fraction of a second when all action stilled. The motion of releasing the bat came to a momentary halt.

This classic action of the batting champion Griffin caught in color. Since the *Globe* wanted only black and white pictures, Griffin put aside the color films of the Rookie of the Year and indeed forgot them for half a century. They had not been duplicated in the intervening years, nor could they be. By the time other photographers thought of filming Williams in color, the youthfulness and innocence was gone, the amiability had diminished, and the .400 hitter had no time to pose for news photographs. The hero had hardened into an icon and the all-American boyishness had given way to a reserved maturity that many thought sullen.

At the moment Griffin photographed Williams in color, he was still called "The Kid." It was not so much his age (he was 19 at the time), but a youthfulness that surrounded him like an aura. He was "the Splendid Splinter."

Later he would become known to the aficionados of baseball as a "four strike hitter." The idea behind the phrase was this: Williams was deemed to have such a good eye judging whether a pitch was a ball or a strike that it was a very confident umpire who would give Williams a called strike. If Williams with his keen eye let the pitch go by . . . well, maybe it was a ball.

That was in mid-career. When the end came, twenty-two years later, John Updike, who is to the world of letters what Ted Williams was to baseball, happened to attend, and then report on, the last game the Splendid Splinter played for the Red Sox. Updike's first-hand story originally appeared in *The New Yorker*. We reprint here but a few pages of "Hub Fans Bid Kid Adieu," eventually published in *Assorted Prose* by John Updike.

"A free-lancer has got to be able to do almost anything . . . . And you've got to be something of an athlete."

Love It or Leave It: Advice of ace color man."
Graphic Graflex News, *March 1949*

Williams was third in the batting order, so he came up in the bottom of the first inning, and Steve Barber, a young pitcher born two months before Williams began playing in the major leagues, offered him four pitches, at all of which he disdained to swing, since none of them were within the strike zone. This demonstrated simultaneously that Williams' eyes were razor-sharp and that Barber's control wasn't. Shortly the bases were full, with Williams on second. "Oh I hope he gets held up at third! That would be wonderful," the girl beside me moaned, and, sure enough, the man at bat walked and Williams was delivered into our foreground. He struck the pose of Donatello's David, the third-base bag being Goliath's head. Fiddling with his cap, swapping small talk with the Oriole third baseman (who seemed delighted to have him drop in), swinging his arms with a sort of prancing nervousness, he looked fine — flexible, hard, and not unbecomingly substantial through the middle. The long neck, the small head, the knickers whose cuffs were worn down near his ankles — all these clichés of sports cartoon iconography were rendered in the flesh.

With each pitch, Williams danced down the baseline, waving his arms and stirring dust, ponderous but menacing, like an attacking goose. It occurred to about a dozen humorists at once to shout, "Steal home! Go, go!" Williams' speed afoot was never legendary. Lou Clinton, a young Sox outfielder, hit a fairly deep fly to center field, Williams tagged up and ran home. As he slid across the plate, the ball, thrown with unusual heft by Jackie Brandt, the Oriole center fielder, hit him on the back.

"Boy, he was really loafing, wasn't he?" one of the collegiate voices behind me said.

"It's cold," the other voice explained, "He doesn't play well when it's cold. He likes heat. He's a hedonist."

The run that Williams scored was the second and last of the inning. Gus Triandos, of the Orioles, quickly evened the score by plunking a home run over the handy left-field wall. Williams, who had had this wall at his back for twenty years, played the ball flawlessly. He didn't budge. He just stood still, in the center of the little patch of grass that his patient footsteps had worn brown, and, limp with lack of interest, watched the ball pass overhead. It was not a very interesting game. Mike Higgins, the Red Sox manager, with nothing to lose, had restricted his major-league players to the left-field line — along with Williams, Frank Malone, a first-rate third baseman, played the game — and had peopled the rest of the terrain with unpredictable youngsters fresh, or not so fresh, off the farms. Other than Williams' recurrent

appearances at the plate, the maladresse of the Sox infield was the sole focus of suspense; the second baseman turned every grounder into a juggling act, while the shortstop did a breathtaking impersonation of an open window. With this sort of assistance, the Orioles wheedled their way into a 4–2 lead. They had early replaced Barber with another young pitcher, Jack Fisher. Fortunately, (as it turned out), Fisher is no cutie; he is willing to burn the ball through the strike zone, and inning after inning this tactic punctured Higgins' string of test balloons.

Whenever Williams appeared at the plate — pounding the dirt from his cleats, gouging a pit in the batter's box with his left foot, wringing resin out of the bat handle with his vehement grip, switching the stick at the pitcher with an electric ferocity — it was like having a familiar Leonardo appear in a shuffle of *Saturday Evening Post* covers. This man, you realized — and here,

perhaps, was the difference, greater than the difference in gifts — really desired to hit the ball. In the third inning, he hoisted a high fly to deep center. In the fifth, we thought he had it; he smacked the ball hard and high into the heart of his power zone, but the deep right field in Fenway and the heavy air and a casual east wind defeated him. The ball died. Al Pilarcik leaned his back against the big "380" painted on the right-field wall and caught it. On another day, in another park, it would have been gone. (After the game, Williams said, "I didn't think I could hit one any harder than that. The conditions weren't good.")

The afternoon grew so glowering that in the sixth inning the arc lights were turned on — always a wan sight in the day time, like the burning headlights of a funeral procession. Aided by the gloom, Fisher was slicing through the Sox rookies, and Williams did not come to bat in the seventh. He was second up in the eighth. This was almost certainly his last time to come to the plate in Fenway Park, and instead of merely cheering, as we had at his three previous appearances, we stood, all of us, and applauded. I had never before heard pure applause in a ballpark. No calling, no whistling, just an ocean of handclaps minute after minute, burst after burst, crowding and running together in continuous succession like the pushes of surf at the edge of the sand. It was a sombre and considered tumult. There was not a boo in it. It seemed to renew itself out of a shifting set of memories as the Kid, the Marine, the veteran of feuds and failures and injuries, the friend of children, and the enduring old pro evolved down the bright tunnel of twenty-two summers toward this moment. At last, the umpire signaled for Fisher to pitch; with the other players, he had been frozen in position. Only Williams had moved during the ovation, switching his bat impatiently, ignoring everything except his cherished task. Fisher wound up, and the applause sank into a hush.

Understand that we were a crowd of rational people. We knew that a home run cannot be produced at will; the right pitch must be perfectly met and luck must ride with the ball. Three innings before, we had seen a brave effort fail. The air was soggy, the season was exhausted. Nevertheless, there will always lurk, around the corner in a pocket of our knowledge of the odds, an indefensible hope, and this was one of the times, which you now and then find in sports, when a density of expectation hangs in the air and plucks an event out of the future.

Fisher, after his unsettling wait, was low with the first pitch. He put the second one over, and Williams swung mightily and missed. The crowd grunted, seeing the classic swing, so long and smooth and quick, exposed. Fisher threw the third time, Williams swung again, and there it was. The ball climbed on a diagonal line into the vast volume of air over center field. From my angle, behind third base, the ball seemed less an object in flight than the tip of a towering, motionless construct, like the Eiffel tower or the Tappan Zee Bridge. It was in the books while it was still in the sky. Brandt ran back to the deepest corner of the outfield grass, the ball descended beyond his reach and struck in the crotch where the bullpen met the wall, bounced chunkily and vanished.

Like a feather caught in a vortex, Williams ran around the square of bases at the center of our beseeching screaming. He ran as he always ran out home runs — hurriedly, unsmiling, head down, as if our praise were a storm of rain to get out of. He didn't tip his cap. Though we thumped, wept and chanted, "We want Ted!" for minutes after he hid in the dugout, he did not come back. Our noise for some seconds passed beyond excitement into a kind of immense open anguish, a wailing, a cry to be saved. But immortality is nontransferable. The papers said that the other players, and even the umpires on the field, begged him to come out and acknowledge us in some way, but he refused. Gods do not answer letters.

❧

Updike's prose caught a crowning moment at the end of a career, just as Griffin's camera had caught the shining beginning. Together they give us the essence of the man, a .400 hitter, hero, and at the end, a reluctant hero, diffident but not disillusioned. Whatever his attitude toward the fans, he loved the game. Griffin's photographs of Williams, in black and white and in color, give us again the hero and the kid who loved the game. "Lost" for fifty years, these photographs of Williams by Griffin are now part of their shared legacy and of the history of baseball and photography.

Ted Williams and Tom Yawkey

INTO THE COMPANY OF THE RENOWNED

Arthur Griffin enjoyed meeting and photographing all people but photographing celebrities — Bostonians, New Englanders and visitors — gave him an opportunity to experience the world at home. Statesmen and world leaders, artists and musicians, actors and "movie stars," politicians, amateur athletes and major sports figures, leaders in industry and education — all found their way to Griffin's lens. Many found their way to his friendship as well.

One story Arthur enjoys recounting involved Charles Boyer, the gifted French actor and screen star, frequently cast as a great lover. Idolized by many women, including Arthur's wife, Claire, he came to Boston along with other celebrities to promote the sale of War Bonds during World War II. Arthur asked to be taken to Mr. Boyer's room and after several photographs had been taken, Arthur told Boyer that his wife was a great fan of his. Would he talk to her on the telephone? "Certainly" said Boyer.

Arthur dialed his home and said to Claire, "Hold on. Charles Boyer wants to speak to you." He handed the phone to Boyer who, in his smooth French accent said, "Mrs. Griffin?" The reply was a raspberry or Bronx cheer blown long and clear along a dozen miles of telephone wire and heard in the room. "Pardon me?" said Boyer. The reply was the same. Arthur took the phone. "That's really Charles Boyer." But Claire, a frequent victim of Arthur's nonsense, had hung up. To prove he had been telling the truth, Arthur had Art Mogur, a well-known Boston publicist, take a picture of Boyer and him together.

Charles Townsend Copeland was, in the first third of the century, one of the most popular teachers at Harvard College, but a man who shunned publicity. When he retired, *Life* called Griffin to take a portrait of him. "Copey's" phone number was unpublished but Griffin, never lacking ingenuity, sent him a telegram reading, "Please call me right off. Important." Copey called and Griffin began to stammer out an explanation. "Arthur Griffin? What class were you in?" Griffin's stammer got worse. "Oh," said Copey, in some exasperation, "Come and see me."

At the door Copey, expecting a former student, saw the camera equipment and said in alarm, "I never pose for pictures. Come in." The whole incident, plus Griffin's persuasiveness, won Copey over. Griffin got the picture, a *Life* exclusive.

Top: *Charles Boyer and Arthur Griffin*. Below: *Charles T. Copeland*

"It's not all wine and roses; but if you love photography, you just take the good with the bad, happy that you are in a profession that beats the outright pursuit of pleasure and is rewarding physically, mentally, and spiritually, and can even be profitable."

Arthur Griffin's New England: The Four Seasons
September 12, 1980

Ethel Barrymore

"On a *Holiday* assignment in the '40s I walked into Ethel Barrymore's dressing room in the Stockbridge Playhouse. She was dressed in a black gown and white cap and was listening to the Red Sox game. She loved the Red Sox and, when I told her about the many times I had photographed Ted Williams and other Red Sox players, we really hit it off. I had her pose as 'Whistler's Mother' as her costume was very much like that of the painter's mother in his famous work. As usual I sent her some pictures. A couple of years later Joe Dineen of the *Globe* got a good story of her at the Ritz, but she wouldn't allow any pictures. I called her and she agreed to be photographed but only if I took the pictures."

Thomas Hart Benton (left) and "model".

"I received an assignment from *Colliers* in 1942 to take pictures of Thomas Hart Benton, one of America's top painters who was in the news with his paintings of the war (World War II). Tom spent long summers on Martha's Vineyard. He was loved by his neighbors and he found them to be wonderful models. He was a fun loving guy and had a small group of friends in for weekly jam sessions. He played the harmonica, his wife the piano, and his 16 year old son, the flute. I got some wonderful photos of Tom and his family including one of his young daughter running naked through the water that became a *Globe* rotocover."

"I always have a camera in my car but the only time I had one in a golf cart was when I was golfing with John Updike. John is a very good golfer. We both love golf and have had a few good arguments over my high handicap . . . I add a stroke for each year of my age over his. He was a young boy when I got most of my pictures of celebrities, but I do like this one I 'sneaked'."

John Updike

Above: *Cardinal Cushing's first formal portrait in his red Cardinal's garb.*
Top right: *President Franklin Roosevelt at the Watertown Arsenal.*
Center right: *Orson Wells at the Colonial Theatre.*
Below right: *Winston Churchill addressing the Mid-Century Convocation during his historic visit to the Massachusetts Institute of Technology.*

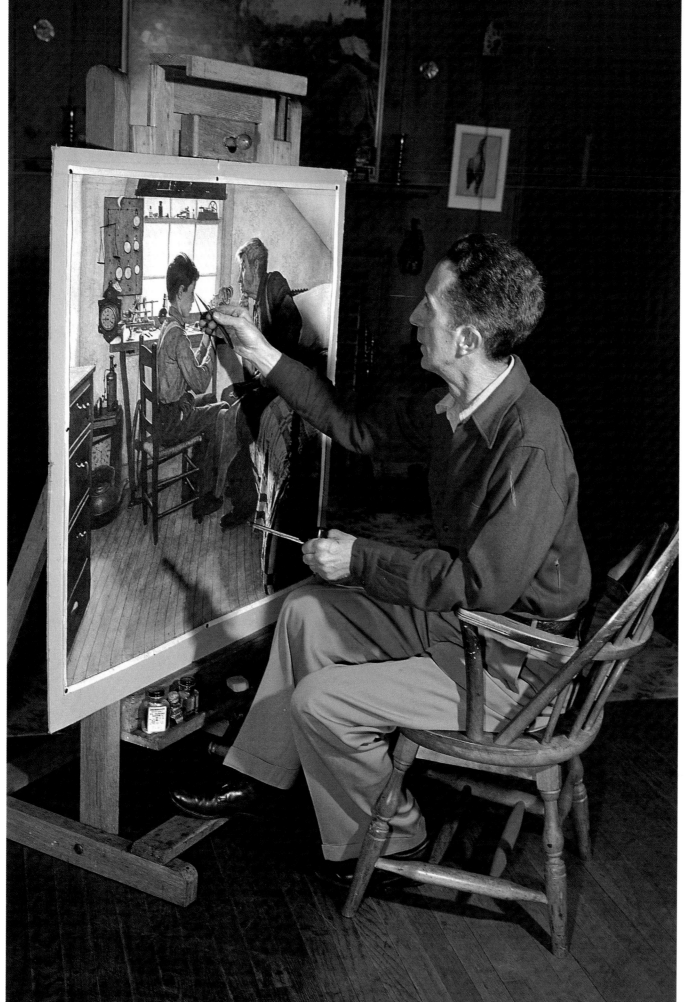

"I first met Norman Rockwell when I drove to Arlington, Vermont, to photograph him for the *Globe*. His new large studio, built across a dirt country road from his old farmhouse, contained costumes of our wars, paintings and other 'props.' Two weeks after my visit, his studio was totally destroyed by fire. Soon after Rockwell bought another old farm in West Arlington a few miles down the Battenkill river and erected another studio behind it. The many times I met with Norman Rockwell I found him to be the most delightful and unspoiled person I have ever known or photographed. When I published my first all-color volume of New England scenes in 1962, he wrote a short essay to accompany my photo of the old covered bridge that he had to drive through to reach his home.

Here is the inscription he wrote and signed on his essay page in my personal copy of that volume."

Dear Mr. Arthur Griffin,
I am proud to be represented in
you truly beautiful book of our
beloved New England. You did
a superb fine job. Sincerely
Norman
Rockwell

Top: *President Hoover*
Bottom: *Betty Davis at the opening celebration of her new film* Dark Victory *in New Hampshire where she maintained a home.*
Right: *Bob Hope and Cary Grant*

Holiday *magazine hired me to photograph Maria Von Trapp and her family in Stowe, Vermont.*

Rocky Marciano, World Heavyweight Boxing Champion, and his family

John Garo. Pre-eminent Boston portrait photographer with whom Griffin studied. He was also the teacher of Yousuf Karsh, currently an esteemed portait photographer.

Young Joe Louis preparing for an early fight.

Frank Sinatra during his first trip to Boston

Gregory Peck and actress in Dennis, Cape Cod.

Elizabeth Taylor in her suite at The Ritz Carlton.

One celebrity who refused to pose for Arthur was Salvador Dali. Arthur, Claire and Lee were traveling in Spain when they found themselves in the small town where the famous painter lived, but learned that he was out fishing. They stopped at a small hotel and, from the balcony of their room, they could look down on Dali's home on the shore. At length they saw the Dali boat come in. Waiting until the great man went inside, they rapped on the door a second time. Dali answered and the Griffins introduced themselves. Dali declined to be photographed saying he had a contract with *Life* that allowed no other pictures but graciously invited them in. Arthur, who had by then severed his connection with *Life*, was particularly impressed with Dali's fishing clothes . . . a business suit with watch and fob chain on his vest.

INTERNATIONAL TRAVEL

Arthur Griffin's love for international travel began during his 1932 trip to Europe. Fortunately for him, he received more and more foreign assignments from such magazines as *Holiday*, *Colliers*, and from Eastman Kodak, assignments that took him to South America, Canada, Europe and Africa.

Griffin's personal and professional trips accelerated from the 1950s through the 1980s when he was usually accompanied by Claire, sometimes Lee their daughter, and later by Polly. The extent of just a few of his trips suggests the scope and depth of the transparencies found in his international collection. Mexico in 1952 for two and a half months and again in 1974 for two months. Europe in 1958 for 127 days, in 1982 for six weeks and again in 1985 for six weeks; five weeks in South America in 1967; the West Indies for five weeks in 1968; and their own Around the World in 82 Days undertaken in 1970.

Many other trips, international and domestic, also combined work, play, peril, enchantment, always adventure and often misadventure . . .

"In January 1968, our African jaunt of 10 weeks took us to a village in Uganda where I was asked to be the judge for a beauty contest. After I had selected the gal on my right as the winner, I was told that her prize was to spend the night with me. For a short while I was in an awful state, until the guide took me aside and told me that I could get out of it by giving the girl's father a few coins.

"During the same trip we were in a small village of Pygmies in Tanzania photographing almost-nude natives when Claire grabbed my arm. 'Arthur, doesn't that jacket look like one of your old ones?' The wearer of it was so small the jacket covered his knees. I went over to him, made apologetic noises and looked at the jacket label. Sure enough, it said 'Zareh of Boston,' a haberdashery near the *Globe* where I used to buy my clothes. Zareh's jackets never gave out and this one I had given away for a foreign missions program."

The Griffin's 82-day trip around the world in 1970 began in Istanbul where they arrived to learn their luggage was lost. They had only their cameras. For four days, they muddled along, prowled the city, and visited the famous Blue Mosque, leaving their shoes outside. They emerged to find their shoes stolen. They tiptoed through icy slush to a taxi. Finally, on the fifth day, their luggage reappeared.

The photographs Griffin shot of the Taj Mahal ended up paying for their entire 82-day trip. Twenty years later, they are still selling. "Now that's a great example of work that has kept me in bread and highballs," says Arthur.

In Kenya, the Griffins stayed at the Mt. Kenya Safari Club of William Holden, the actor, and enjoyed his personal luxury suite with a large television set. Curiously there was, at that time, no television in Kenya. A show that could be bettered by any television, however, was always to be found outside their window, doorway, tent flap, or cheesecloth.

"Either you love photography, can't get enough of it, or you ought to leave it alone. A good photographer doesn't need to be prodded to keep going."

Love It or Leave It: Advice of ace color man."
Graphic Graflex News, *March 1949*

Cholula, Mexico, Church of San Francisco, 1952

"For our trip to Mexico in 1952 we took our new canvas top convertible Ford with their first automatic shift. When we arrived in Mexico City we took the car into the main Ford Agency for an oil change and quick tune-up, work requiring perhaps a few hours. When I returned for it the same day, the automatic shift and parts were on the floor of the big garage. The guys just took it apart for the hell of it to see how it worked. It took them two days to solve the jig-saw puzzle. From then on, throughout our trip, every time we started the car until it automatically shifted into drive, it shook and sounded as if it would fall apart. We didn't dare take it to a garage again. After many weeks and many thousand miles, we returned to Texas and immediately went to another Ford agency. It took them just a few minutes to make all the adjustments."

Nazare, Portugal, 1958

Moscow, Russia, St. Basil's Cathedral, 1969

New Delhi, India, Taj Mahal, 1970

In India, the Griffins' travel agent wired them not to go to Nepal because the king had taken over all the hotel rooms in the country to accommodate guests for his son's wedding. Such a warning only aroused Griffin's journalistic instinct. So off they went to Nepal. They found themselves without quarters but found themselves at a cocktail party where a familiar voice hailed "Arthur Griffin." It was Lowell Thomas, world-famous author and radio celebrity whom Griffin had met many times skiing in Vermont. Thomas got them accommodations and arranged for Griffin to get all the pictures he wanted.

Cambodia, Angkor Wat, 1970

As the Griffin's around-the-world trip continued, news from Cambodia warned of a military coup and discouraged travel. Griffin was convinced that if he didn't get to Cambodia then, he would never get to photograph the famous ruins of Angkor Wat. When they arrived at Phnom Penh it was evident that all was not well. They were meticulously searched and questioned at length by customs' officials. Griffin, apprehensive lest they accidentally expose films he had taken or even seize them, threatened publicity of the worst sort in international publications. The next day found Arthur touring the city and photographing freely.

At noon they left for Angkor Wat, arrived without incident and had three glorious days photographing the ancient, splendid ruins. Griffin's instinct told him not to return to Phnom Penh. Again the Griffin luck held and they were able to fly instead to Hong Kong. There the next day, while having breakfast, they read that the political coup had indeed taken place. The Griffins had been on the last plane out.

Portofino, Italy, 1982

Sveti Sjefin, Yugoslavia, 1985

NEW ENGLAND NOSTALGIA

In September, 1962, the first all color photographic book on New England was published by Arthur Griffin. *New England* was an immediate photographic, artistic and financial success. It set the standard for all classic color New England landscapes for years to come and furthered Griffin's reputation as a major pioneer in the field of color landscape photography. The copy on the book's jacket summarized well the origins of the talent and the drive of the man who had become identified with the romantic, classic New England landscape. "Arthur Griffin had a number of things going for him when he decided to take up photography seriously. His number one asset was his intense interest in art, his very real ability as an artist and his keen sense of composition . . . . Couple those assets with Arthur's tremendous energy and patience and you have an unbeatable combination. He can wait, day after day, for just that right type of lighting. He sometimes drives 200 and 300 miles a day through what the ordinary person would consider the very peak of photogenic scenery without seeing the kind of picture he wants. Today he shoots only color and he probably has the finest and most complete file of New England in existence. The samples in this magnificent book are just that; wonderful color studies of every phase of New England scenery."

In December, 1959, *Yankee* Magazine had commissioned an article by Griffin, "My Favorite Ten" in which Griffin, "photographer extraordinary, takes you to his ten favorite spots in New England." Also appearing in the magazine was the first color photograph to appear in *Yankee*. Robb Sagendorph, publisher, recognized Griffin's work and began to run a double-spread of a Griffin photograph each month. Arthur was still thinking "book" and, with Sagendorph, planned on publication. It was agreed that each month 15,000 extra prints of each double-spread would be printed. By 1962 more than half a million color prints were ready.

" . . . New England offers more for artists, photographers and lovers of beauty than any other section of its size in the world. We really have just about everything . . . . Where is Fall more colorful? Coastline more interesting? Spring more awakening? Summer more delightful and changeable? Winter more photogenic (and cold)?"

"My 10 Favorite Photogenic Spots in New England"
Yankee *Magazine, December 1959*

NEW ENGLAND

original essays by

Joseph Chase Allen • Faith Baldwin
Elswyth Thane Beebe
Alton Hall Blackington
Henry Beston • Hal Borland
Thornton W. Burgess
Margaret Bourke-White
Erwin D. Canham • Al Capp
Gladys Hasty Carroll
Mary Ellen Chase
Elizabeth Coatsworth
Francis W. Dahl • Eleanor Early
Claude Moore Fuess • Robert Frost*
Edmund Gilligan • John Gould
Walter Hard • Ralph Nading Hill
Stewart H. Holbrook
Henry Beetle Hough • George Howe
Herbert A. Kenny
Louise Andrews Kent
Frances Parkinson Keyes
Louis M. Lyons • David McCord
Peter Greene Morison
Marjorie Mills • Vrest Orton
Daniel J. O'Brien
David Patten • Haydn S. Pearson
Horace Reynolds • Benjamin M. Rice
Louise Dickinson Rich
Doc Rockwell • Norman Rockwell
Edward Rowe Snow
W. A. Swanberg • Edwin Way Teale
Newton F. Tolman • Edward Weeks
Frederic F. Van de Water
Laurence L. Winship
Elizabeth Yates
*from ''In the Clearing''©

full color photographs by **ARTHUR GRIFFIN**

edited by **ROBB SAGENDORPH**

Dedication: "To Claire . . . The Best Camera Caddy in the World."

Griffin had for years been planning the book. But at the last minute, Griffin and Sagendorph, two opinionated Yankees, could not agree on marketing strategies. Griffin bought out control of the proposed book. Their friendship remained, however, and Sagendorph served as the editor of what was to be simply titled, *New England* . . . the first full color pictorial book of New England landscapes. This was to be a simple but elegant book. The prints were 9 by 12 inches, each tipped in on gray laid paper, all hand-bound. Forty-eight of the prints were sent to 48 New England authors, many of them either personal friends or people who had been photographed by Griffin. They were asked to write a brief essay to accompany the print.

The cover photograph would be of Stark, New Hampshire, the first color photograph to appear in *Yankee*. The cover would list the names of the authors, a virtual roll call of New England's outstanding literary names of the time. But there was still the question of a title.

"We needed a title . . . so I offered a free book to friends who could come up with something brilliant. An old codger in Vermont suggested 'New England Beautiful' but in the end we settled for *New England*. At the same time, another old Yankee, once promotion manager for the *Globe* and later for the Ford Motor Company, wrote to say that he could only afford half the $15.00 price tag on the book. I decided to give him and the Vermonter half a book each. So I went to the bindery and asked the manager to cut one of the books in half, length-wise. 'Sacrilege!' he said and refused to do it. So I took a copy and did it myself. I sent half to the old Yankee along with a bill for $7.50. He paid. Then I sent the other half to the codger who had come up with half the name."

Publishing as *An Arthur Griffin Book*, the new publishers Arthur and Claire, after handling the whole business of publishing, turned to another old friend, Houghton Mifflin, for promotion and sales. Sales were brisk and by early November Arthur put in an order for a second printing. As Griffin recounts, "Suddenly the roof fell in. Books began to be returned from the stores. Doubleday returned 300. The complaint was that the pages were buckling, and they were. The bindery, in tipping in the pages, had pasted down three corners and when the gray paper dried, the colored print buckled." The bindery and Arthur both learned the art of hand-tipping at the same time. The problem was solved and the book went on to three more printings.

Letters of congratulations poured in for *New England*. Ansel Adams, the famous black and white landscape photographer, wrote in admiration not alone of the photographs but at the publishing enterprise that brought the book into being. The book received several awards, many excellent reviews and congratulations from throughout the world. Today *New England* is a collector's item.

Robb Sagendorph in front of early office of *The Old Farmer's Almanac*, 1950.

Top: *Lithographers and Printers National Association, Inc. Lithographic Awards Competition and Exhibit, 1963*
"To: Arthur Griffin, designer, art director and photographer
 And: Forbes Lithographic Manufacturing Company
 For: *New England*"
Bottom: *Lowell Thomas, world-famous author and radio celebrity, enjoys* New England *at a gathering of skimeisters in Stowe, Vermont.*

ARTHUR GRIFFIN'S

NEW ENGLAND REVISITED

ARTHUR GRIFFIN'S
NEW ENGLAND REVISITED

With descriptions chosen & edited by DAVID McCORD

ARTHUR GRIFFIN

Dedication: "Affectionately dedicated to My daughter LEE who designed this Book for Me."

The reception for and success of *New England* naturally stimulated the desire for a much larger and more ambitious venture, *New England Revisited*. The week the book was to hit the bookstores, *The Boston Globe* printed a twelve-page color supplement announcing its availability on September 12, 1966 and providing a look at twelve prints from the book. Among the many laudatory reviews, one by Victor O. Jones in the *Globe* was Arthur's favorite. We quote but one column of three.

"The last time I happened to be walking along the Boylston St. shopping area, I was startled to see a window of Shreve Crump and Low, the jewelers, filled with nothing but copies of a large book.

"Since when, I wondered, have Shreve, Crump and Low been in the book-selling business? The answer is that this is the very first time. But it's not likely to be the last time — not if Arthur Griffin continues to put together such jewels as the one that filled Shreve's window. It's a beautiful, beautiful

book called *New England Revisited*, some 200 pages of superb color photographs of New England scenes at all seasons, taken, of course, by Griffin. To complement the pictures there are suitable passages from the writings of 62 famous authors, selected by David McCord, ranging all the way from the 17th century William Bradford to Rachel Carson. The volume, about 14 by 12, is designed by Griffin's daughter, Lee. All the mechanics such as paper, covers, binding, printing are custom-produced in these parts under the personal supervision of ole Arthur.

"The man is, of course, a great artist, but he is also a superb technician in anything involving photography, paper, print, and book-making in general. He also backs his taste and judgment in the highly competitive field of publishing with his own money. His darkrooms are in his modest Winchester home and the publishing part of his enterprise seems to be stored inside his Tyrolean hat.

"The only facet of picture-book publishing in which he apparently lacks confidence is the actual, literary editing. But for that purpose he's simplified matters by engaging the very best there is — David McCord (the distinguished Boston author and poet) . . ."

The success of *New England* and *New England Revisited* heightened Arthur's confidence in the value of his work, and in his own business judgments. Pleased that his work had achieved a measure of significance and acceptance, he and Claire decided to publish a third book. But Claire soon became too ill to provide her usual vigor to the project and Arthur quietly

Arthur Griffin and Governor of Massachusetts, John Volpe.

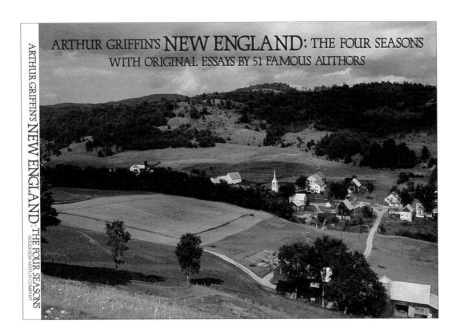

Dedication: "To Polly, my wife. She came with a casserole and stayed for dinner."

shelved the book while he tended Claire in her long illness. Her death robbed him of his enthusiasm for another publication and for several years he thought no more about the book.

Then in 1980, *Arthur Griffin's New England: The Four Seasons* was finally published by Houghton Mifflin with a dedication "To Polly, my wife. She came with a casserole and stayed for dinner."

Polly had entered Arthur's life at an important time for both of them, at a time when she too would become Arthur's wife and partner, travel companion, fellow artist and writer.

The ingredients of all three books were to remain basically the same; the design, by Arthur's daughter Lee, designer of the first two volumes, was still simple and elegant; Griffin's classic and romantic New England landscapes were paired with an essay by a distinguished writer, many of whom had become Arthur's friends; a footnote by Arthur provided technical and anecdotal detail about each photograph. *Four Seasons* also included a small black and white photograph of a comparable scene, taken by Claire . . . a tribute to her and an integral part of the design of the book and of their life together.

In the pages that follow you'll find but a few of Arthur Griffin's favorite photographs of New England. All of them are early Griffin classics, taken by the journalist, artist and technician who understood and loved composition, color, and the changing seasons and land of New England; taken by the man who said in 1980, "I know New England like a book."

Polly and Arthur, 1980

Stonington, Connecticut, 1970s

Isabella Stuart Gardner Museum, Boston. Early 1940s

President Ike Eisenhower fishing at Little Boy Falls in Maine.

Snug Harbor, Rhode Island, 1955

Massachusetts State House, Boston, 1942

Gloucester, Massachusetts, 1939

Grafton, Vermont, 1962

Lower Waterford, Vermont, 1960

Perkins Cove, Ogunquit, Maine, 1955

Turbots Creek, Kennebunkport, Maine, 1940

Martha's Vineyard, Menemsha, Massachusetts, 1940

Brant Point Light, Nantucket, Massachusetts. Early 1980s

High Tide, Low Tide, Lubec, Maine, 1960s